And I Prayed...

Cathy Jo Schroeder-Soden

Fulton Books, Inc.
Meadville, PA

Published by Fulton Books 2021

ISBN 978-1-63860-323-8 (paperback)
ISBN 978-1-63860-324-5 (digital)

Printed in the United States of America

This book and story are dedicated to my late husband, Paul Joseph Schroeder, who succumbed to kidney cancer at the age of forty-six after a three-and-a-half-year battle. He gave permission before he died to share his story and his testimony. Our daughters were aged ten and seven when he died and have been exposed to some life trials that have changed them and matured them in ways beyond their individual years. While this is Paul's story, it is also our story as a family. It details our journey through marital trials and health trials and how we have changed and grown and have come full circle to love again.

Contents

Prologue

Early to mid-January 2013, Paul called me into the bathroom because he was urinating blood. He insisted he must have a kidney stone, since it was common after having gastric sleeve surgery (which he underwent, against my objections, in September 2012). I examined him and told him he did not have a kidney stone and that he needed to call his provider in the morning to get a urinalysis done. He shrugged me off saying, "Nah, it will get better." And it did, until it happened again, and then a third time.

When this occurred, I was an RN with a master's in science in nursing and was a family nurse practitioner. I had been an RN for twenty-two years, working as a family nurse practitioner for thirteen of those years, with emergency room experience. As an experienced nurse, I can spot a patient with a kidney stone from across the room. He did not have a kidney stone. At all. Not even a small one. But he felt he knew more, even though he was a blue-collar, jack-of-all-trades-master-of-none guy. His words to describe himself, not mine. He asked for nursing advice all the time, just would not follow it, or relished in telling me that I was wrong. It was not the first time he denied my clinical experience, and unfortunately for him, he was always the one who was wrong.

For example, he woke me up one night with abdominal pain and diarrhea. I quickly palpated his abdomen and thought he probably had appendicitis. He told me I was wrong. So I told him to wake me if it got worse and proceeded to go back to sleep, since it was around 2:00 a.m. He called out from work but did not admit that he was feeling worse until he sheepishly called me at work at 11:00 a.m. from the emergency room asking me, "What surgeon should I ask for? I have appendicitis."

The bloody urine, or hematuria, slowly cleared over the next two to three days, and he never called his health care provider for an evaluation. Then the hematuria started again around April, lasted a few days, and cleared. Again, he declined to go to his provider for a urine test to detect any microscopic hematuria (blood in the urine only seen under microscopic examination). The third time really got his attention as the bleeding was worse, and he was passing clots of blood. Now he was scared and willing to listen. He agreed to see a urologist, and he was able to quickly get an appointment. I, of course, went with him. The urologist, who shall not be named, ordered the diagnostic tests appropriate for the problem but never examined him. The appointment occurred from across a desk with no physical exam performed. I was puzzled and not impressed with this doctor, but the tests that I knew needed to be done had been ordered.

I had discussed with Paul the differential diagnoses, or list of possible problems, that could cause the hematuria. This included the possibility of cancer. I told him of my experience in having several patients diagnosed with bladder cancer due to microscopic blood found on routine urinalysis. I was heavily leaning toward this diagnosis, as was the urologist. We would both be wrong.

Paul went for a CAT scan of his abdomen, July 22, 2013, and had instructed the radiology office to copy the results to my office. The office staff placed the report off to the side of the desk. They saw the result summary and were hoping to delay me seeing the report. I remember grabbing the report and even saying, "Wow, that was quick."

I started to read it as I walked back down the office hallway, and then I gasped and starting to hyperventilate. I slid down the wall onto the floor. I am not one for being overly dramatic, but the report shocked me. The office staff started crying, knowing what the report stated, and I remember one of them crying, "Oh, CJ."

One of them called for Dr. B who fortunately was present in the office with me that day. I was up and walking but shaking. I shared the report with him. It showed a cancerous mass but not the bladder cancer that I was expecting. It was a 12.3-cm mass in his right kidney consistent with cancer and was pressing upward against the liver and a second smaller mass in the lower part of the kidney. I worked in an ENT office, and three-centimeter masses in the neck or throat area are considered large, so a twelve-centimeter mass was huge (2.54 centimeter equals one inch so this was close to five inches). The tumor was almost as large as the kidney itself.

Dr. B wanted to send me home as I was clearly not in a good frame of mind to continue to treat patients, but I really did not want to go home. I do not have a poker face, and Paul would immediately know something was wrong. I did not want to be the one to tell him the results. My boss looked at the name of the ordering physician of the scan and told me that I had to tell him because "that doctor has the bedside manner of a flea!"

I remained at work to keep myself distracted and delay the inevitable. I used my lunch break to call the urology department at the Hospital of University of Pennsylvania (HUP), not expecting to get an appointment for a few weeks. I was very pleasantly surprised to find they had an opening for the end of the week. Today was a Monday, and they offered me an appointment for Friday. I finished my workday early and headed home. And I prayed for strength as I drove home. I also prayed and thanked God for the fast appointment.

As soon as I walked in the door, Paul asked if I had gotten the results. I told him that yes, I did get the results. He followed me into the kitchen. I was leaning against the counter for support as I started to tell him the results. He kept talking over me. I do not think he even heard that it was not bladder cancer but rather a kidney tumor. I told him I made him an appointment at HUP for Friday and that he most likely would need to have surgery to remove his entire kidney. He kept talking over me and around me and was not really paying attention until the words "You need to have the kidney removed," finally registered. Then he took a breath and really looked at me, pulled out a chair, and told me to "start over and tell me again."

This was the beginning of the cancer journey for him but also the beginning of a few years of multiple health issues. Paul was forty-three years old. Kidney cancer tends to affect men more than women but usually later in life. The fact he was much younger than the normal age generally tends to mean a more aggressive version of the disease.

The years ensuing from 2013 through 2018 would entail his progression of disease despite multiple experimental and non-experimental therapies; additional surgeries (2014, 2015); finding me unconscious from a seizure due to a noncancerous brain tumor and subsequent brain surgery (February 2015); then one month later, his own brain surgery due to his cancer; entering hospice October 2016; his death in February 2017; and then my own cancer diagnosis one year later. This story is one of hope, resilience, perseverance, and faith. We demonstrated to our children how to support each other in the marriage vows of "sickness and in health" literally, and they witnessed the changes in their dad, as he found stability, received the gift of faith, and came to know Jesus Christ as his Lord and Savior. He became more present with us and became a better husband and father, and we formed a stronger family unit through these challenges. We were the recipients of so much emotional and spiritual support and could see the many blessings that came to us despite the trials. I have dedicated a chapter at the end of the book to discussing these blessings that were bestowed on us. It was easier to discuss them altogether instead of weaving them into the story individually as they happened. I pray this chronicle of our journey encourages you in your own trials and your personal walk in faith.

"For I am the Lord your God who takes hold of your right hand and says to you, do not fear, I will help you" (Is. 41:13 NIV). This is just one of many verses I looked up on fear in the Bible during these years. Fear is mentioned in some form over 300 times in the Bible. Our suffering may seem meaningless to us at times, but in His providence it is not. He gets the glory when a person is miraculously healed, and He gets the glory when someone develops faithfulness and character through suffering. This is our story of our journey in and to Christ and how He provided for us through this journey. I prayed before, during, and after writing this that He would give me the words and strength to share Paul's testimony in a way that honored Paul's memory and was delivered in a way that he would be proud of. Most importantly, I prayed that this story gives glory to God. In the words of one of my favorite Christian artists, Toby Mac, "Use this testimony for Your glory, here I am Lord, steal my show."

Chapter 1

Paul and I met in high school, junior year, and disliked each other immediately. I thought he was a grease shop monkey, and he thought I was a "curly-haired, permed prissy girl" (this was the late '80s!). But through some mutual friends, our paths kept crossing, and we started dating midway through our senior year, attending senior prom together and graduating together in 1989. We grew up in the suburbs outside of Trenton, New Jersey, in solid middle-class families. My dad was a blue-collar worker; his dad was a policeman and the notorious Officer Friendly in our town. Both our moms worked for the State of New Jersey. He has two brothers, and I have two sisters and a brother.

He proposed in 1992 when I finished nursing school, and we married October 8, 1994. During the next eight years, we lived in an apartment and had dogs and boats and came and went as we pleased.

I returned to school and completed my bachelor of science in nursing in 1997. By then, I was employed at Hahnemann University in Philadelphia and started my graduate program through their school (which is now Drexel). I completed the family nurse practitioner program/master of science in nursing in 2000.

Paul started working as a municipal worker for our township. He moved around a bit in various positions and went back to vocational school. He got a certificate in maintenance repair and electric, but he never wanted to complete the apprenticeship for the electrician certification. While not glamorous, the pay was decent, the hours were good, and the benefits were fabulous. While I worked my way up in nursing degrees and held various nursing titles, he also worked his way up the ladder at work. He became involved in the union and was president of the union for the township. This led to him being offered a job as a union representative, and he then represented blue-collar employees in other municipalities. He became well-versed in civil service law and contract negotiations. He became very respected in the job because he was passionate about it.

In 2003, we purchased our first house, a modest three-bedroom ranch. At the time, we had no children and had no real plans for children. We had our dogs and our boat and were very content. Paul became very immersed in all aspects of boating, and our weekends were spent at the marina, regardless of the weather. We made several boating trips down the Jersey coast, across the Delaware Bay into the Chesapeake Bay to explore on summer vacations. Each trip was fantastic. We made so many memories with our boating excursions on both Barnegat Bay and Chesapeake Bay.

Then the biological clock started ticking, as Paul joked. In December 2004, we welcomed our first child Kiersten, and in January 2009, Kaylee. They grew up on the weekends at the marina, boating and swimming in Barnegat Bay. But Paul did not really embrace being a father. Sure, he loved his girls, but he resented me for the changes it made in our life. We still did all the things with the kids that we did before they came into our lives; it just took more time, planning, and effort. Later, he realized and admitted that he resented that my time and attention were focused on the kids and taken off him. He felt like he no longer had his "best friend."

This was the start of a downward spiral in our marriage. Paul had a non-treated mood disorder that caused cyclical bouts of depression. He had depression and cutting issues as a teen that were not addressed fully. He did receive treatment as a young adult due to a driving under the influence charge at the age of twenty-two. This was a big turning point for him. He continued antidepressants for many years but still had mood swings. Over the years, because of not being properly treated, the mood swings became worse. It caused him to have a skewed view of life and an inability to appreciate the many good things we had. I felt content with what I had in life, he was not and could not understand why I did not want "more." That "more" to him was more materialistic things, more tools, more boats and four-wheelers and newer cars. Nothing was ever enough, and he was only satisfied for a short period.

Having children and wanting them baptized got me back into the church. I had taken myself to church during my childhood and teen years with a family that lived at the end of my street and whose daughter I went to school with. By the time Paul and I met, I was not attending church, and while he knew I had been "religious," it was not a part of my life during the first ten years of our marriage. I continued to pray, but not regularly and did not belong to a church. Paul was not a Christian and was adamant that he believed in evolution and the Big Bang theory. He thought there had to be a God but that was the extent of his belief. He was okay with me taking the kids to church as it got him out of "dad duty," but as he saw changes in me (not sure what he saw) and my involvement in church activities increase, his resentment for my church attendance grew. I sent our kids to Faith Christian School for preschool and kept them there for elementary school. Sometimes he was onboard with it as he admitted the curriculum was good and the teachers were "good people," and sometimes he was against it due to the theological teachings. He did sometimes voice his displeasure in the Bible teachings for the kids, stating they were being brainwashed, but I felt that it was money well spent. I worked, and this is where I wanted to invest my money. I argued that he was not involved in school, homework, or classroom activities, and if he wanted a say in what school they went to, then he needed to step up and become involved with school-related activities, not just show up for the school musicals.

As his mood disorder became more unstable, his anger and resentment grew, which led me to grow in anger and resentment toward him. There were many times that we would talk things out, but his professions of love for me never matched his actions. His negative words and withdrawal of affection and silent treatments were not the actions of a man who loved me unconditionally and who professed, "I would walk through fire for you." I knew he loved me, but I often felt abandoned more times than not and certainly felt like a single parent despite his physical presence. My breaking point came when Kiersten was just six years old, and she asked me why I was always mad at daddy. She would always get upset when Paul and I argued, and we were arguing more often, but I did not realize the impact it was having on her.

I decided I did not want her to think this was how a marital relationship should be. I wanted her to witness two people showing affection for each other and showing a united front in all things related to our family and our home. We rarely showed affection in front of the kids because of our mutual anger. I took them everywhere with me and planned weekend activities that Paul rarely participated in with us, despite the girls asking him to come along, even during the winter when the boat was dry-docked. The happiest times of connection for us as a family was the summer weekends at the boatyard. But these weekends were also hard. It was a lot of work to pack up kids and dogs and a camper and take it to the marina and back each weekend and clean it all back up Sunday afternoons. Unfortunately, his behavior and sometimes negative words regarding having children were observed and heard by our fellow boating friends. This resulted in their own anger toward him—something I learned about later.

He was quite capable of taking care of the girls on his own and did a great job of it. I dropped them off to school, he picked them up and got them settled after school until I got home from work. He was quite capable with many things—a jack-of-all-trades guy—except mental illness prevented him from being the man, husband, and father that I knew he could be. I told my sister-in-law, Lori, that mental illness was like a mistress in our marriage. It was like there were three people in the marriage; me, him, and his mental illness.

I would hear from others how he was proud of me and his girls and talked about us all the time. However, he was not able to say those same kind words directly to us. As I already stated, I knew he loved me and his girls and that is what kept me in the relationship for so long, but always hoping and praying that things would be better with him. I prayed, often, that God would help him fight back whatever demons were in his head, or knock him over the head with a 2x4, if that would put some sense in him. I prayed this many times over the years, and God would eventually answer it through the most unexpected circumstances.

Chapter 2

I gave him an ultimatum of getting the correct mental health help that he needed or pack his bags and get out. I gave him three months to find and begin some type of therapy. We had attended couples counseling about two years prior but did not get too far. It was always the same issues and complaints without any resolution because I was content with all that we had in life and found our kids to be a blessing. He found the kids to be a disruption to his lifestyle and was never satisfied with all the things we had.

And we had a lot—a nice home, two new cars, two dogs, two beautiful daughters, a boat, and a camper. And then he had to have a quad and more and more and more. He felt that if I was able to pay the bills then it was okay to keep spending. He would not consider getting rid of any of the toys despite not having any money in savings for emergencies. We should have had money saved—we made enough with two salaries—but every bit of it was allotted to make payments on our "stuff." It bothered me, that at our age and place in our careers, that we lived so tightly because of this. He did not see it the same way.

Something in my tone, my facial expression or stance, made an impact as he knew I was serious in my decision. Something somehow clicked that this was serious. He then went into a quick and severe depression, despite him being on an antidepressant. He had suicide ideation but did not qualify for crisis admission (go figure), and it took several days of phone calls, by both of us, to find a psychiatric provider to accept him for an evaluation. It was scary and frustrating, but we did finally get a return phone call.

We found a psychiatric nurse practitioner that was fee-for-service only. I did not know her personally but knew of her through mutual colleagues. At this point, the money was secondary to getting him treatment. She was awesome. She immediately identified him as being bipolar II and placed him on a mood-stabilizing drug. He had weekly counseling appointments, and she called him out on his behaviors and thought processes. I cannot begin to truly describe the changes in his personality, but the most profound was his repentance of his harsh words and lack of actions pertaining to our relationship and our family.

He was not willing to sell any of the toys to lighten our financial burden, but he was at least more appreciative of the possessions we had. Between the medication and counseling, his thought processes changed. He heard what I was saying instead of my words being twisted in his head and taken in a completely different meaning. He started spending more time with us and making time for our girls. They noticed, even at their young ages.

Thankfully, this course of events occurred the summer of 2012. Through weekly counseling and appropriate medication therapy, he was in a much better and stable mental state when he got the cancer diagnosis. Things may have been much different otherwise.

I, too, started to see a therapist once he got stabilized. She helped me to address my own anger and resentment toward him and to deconstruct my protective walls. I had to learn how to identify triggers; otherwise, old habits of coping would reemerge. I had to learn to not take on the problems of friends or family and to separate myself from the outside drama, which is hard when you are in the helping/healing profession. But for my own sanity, it had to be done as I had enough drama occurring under my own roof. This therapy then turned into anticipatory grief therapy, after he was diagnosed with the cancer.

Chapter 3

On Friday, July 26, 2013, we met with the urologist at HUP. He reviewed the scans and told Paul he needed to remove the entire kidney. Paul was to have a radical nephrectomy on August 7, 2013. It all happened very quickly, for which we were grateful. He was admitted the day before the surgery and underwent a procedure where the blood flow to the kidney was destroyed, effectively "killing the kidney" which greatly reduces blood loss during the operation. On the morning of his procedure, and again the next morning before his actual surgery, I prayed for our safety in traveling to and from the hospital as well as caring, competence, and compassion of his treating team of physicians and nurses and full removal of the cancer.

The entire kidney, and the cancer, were removed without any complications. He did amazingly well through the surgery and was discharged home five days later. His stay at HUP was uneventful, and the care he received from the nursing staff was excellent. My prayers had been answered.

I generally try to stay under the radar with my profession. When a staff nurse finds out that I have advanced degrees in nursing, it tends to make them feel like they are being watched and back in nursing school again. I try hard to just let them do their job and stay out of their way. I will not say anything if the job is being done properly.

Paul felt differently and kept nothing to himself, despite me asking him not to say anything. He especially waited for me to arrive at the hospital to bathe him and get him up telling the nursing staff that "my wife, a nurse, will do it." I never let on about my education when I attended physician visits with Paul, but since it is ingrained in me, my ease in use of medical terminology and procedures would give me away. If that did not clue them in, then Paul would tell them what my occupation was as he liked to think it kept them honest!

The first night of his hospital stay, my pastor, Pastor Emmons, visited with Paul to offer spiritual support. This visit was unexpected as Paul had attended my church maybe two times to see Kiersten perform in a kid's choir program. This visit was, despite Paul's lack of religious belief, much appreciated. He was humbled that my pastor came out to visit him and respected him even more for it.

Paul's depression and mood disorder were under good control at this time, otherwise, I am not sure if he would have coped with his diagnosis as well as he did. I feared he would have curled up into a ball and slept his life away and given up. Instead, he embraced it, was empowered to manage his care, and researched all he could about his diagnosis and possible treatments and became his own advocate.

After meeting the surgeon at HUP, Paul started researching facts about kidney cancer. He needed something to keep him occupied, and it helped him feel in control. However, we did not know what type of cancer he had yet, so he could not focus on any one type. I felt it more beneficial to find out the exact tumor type and then research it specifically, not generally. Different personalities, different approaches. He needed to find out what he could, and I had to let him. After the surgery, when we got the pathology report, he was then able to focus his search to his type of kidney cancer. There is a plethora of information on it, but unfortunately, there was not any new or great improvements in its management. Still, knowledge is power, and I encouraged him to learn as much as he could. It would serve us well as we were our own advocates for his care.

Over the past year, he also became a more devoted father and more attentive husband. Both of which were already improved due to his better mental health, but he now started to value all he had so much more. Again, I felt my prayers had been answered. His mental demons were identified and were being excised. He was finding some peace. I prayed for continued peace and continued freedom from those mental demons as well as a good outcome medically.

A few weeks later, we met with the renal oncologist (kidney cancer doctor) at HUP. She was very experienced and had spent the prior two decades at Fox Chase Cancer Center. Paul's pathology report stated some aggressive characteristics of his cancer, but it was a common variant of kidney cancer—clear cell cancer. He was staged at 2B, no lymph nodes involved and no metastasis (spread of disease), but it had invaded into a blood vessel which made it a little worse. Due to this invasion, and the size of his tumor, he had a 70 percent chance of this coming back within the next five years. What we found out, on our own, is that kidney cancer tumors greater than 3 cm always metastasize, and his initial tumor was 12 cm! No treatment, beyond surgery, is usually offered or necessary at stages 1 or 2. Medical therapy is reserved for more advanced cases at stages 3 and 4. There is no traditional chemotherapy for kidney cancer, and some scans are not done as kidney cancer does not show well on them (PET scans which are standard in staging of other cancers).

The medications available were relatively new, within the prior five to six years and were targeted to stage 3 or 4 kidney cancers. They did not cure it but would stabilize the tumors—termed "progression-free survival"—for up to seven months before a change would be required. Some people got much longer results. He would not be a candidate ordinarily; however, there was a clinical trial enrolling these earlier-staged cancers to see if treatment would prevent or delay recurrence of disease. It was a double-blinded placebo-controlled trial called EVEREST. This meant he was randomly assigned to either a sugar pill or the real pill and no one would know which it was. Well, due to side effects, we figured it out quickly that he was on the real drug.

He had scans done in October before starting the trial to verify no evidence of disease and would be scanned again in three-month increments for the duration of the trial. He got repeat scans done February 17, 2014, which showed a mass on his left adrenal gland—which was present on the prior scan but not commented on, suspicious for cancer but not certain,—and five new tumors in his left kidney, all consistent with cancer. Yes, five new tumors, while on a drug used to treat kidney cancer. Stunned and shaken, we wanted to know how and what do we do now. And I prayed for comfort, healing, and relief of our anxiety, answers, and a good treatment plan.

Chapter 4

The oncologist "unblinded" the study to verify that Paul was indeed on the real drug. These tumors needed to be biopsied to confirm that they were the same type of cancer. This was an outpatient procedure and scheduled in November.

The new tumors were biopsied at HUP and were confirmed to be the same type of cancer. While we waited for the surgery, we were scared and nervous. I started to pray silently at his bedside. Maybe I should have prayed out loud. I was a Christian but not comfortable in my faith yet and not comfortable praying out loud. I thought I needed that "prayer-ese" language, but now I realize how stupid that is. You do not need special words or to sound a certain way when you pray, you need only to pray. Paul had questions that I did not have answers to, but he was interested. I had a pamphlet in my purse from church that my pastor used to evangelize so I pulled it out and read it to him. It gave us both some comfort.

Paul was sent for genetic testing to look for certain chromosome mutations. He now had bilateral kidney cancer, which usually means a hereditary/genetic mutation. He tested negative for all of them. The oncologist could not explain why Paul had bilateral kidney cancer in the absence of any genetic abnormalities.

She then referred us out of HUP to Fox Chase Cancer Center to see Dr. U., a urological (kidney/bladder) surgeon. She felt his expertise was unmatched in doing surgery to try to save the left kidney. I was quite impressed that she was sending us out of her hospital network for care but she felt it was in Paul's best interest to do so.

We met with Dr. U. about two weeks later. He told us that the kidney cancer tumors generally grow slow, and this should just be monitored for now. He did not want to rush into surgery until the tumors got closer to the three-centimeter size. While we appreciated not being rushed into surgery, we did not feel optimistic regarding the "slow growth" of kidney cancer tumors since these were not present three months ago and were already measuring 1.9 cm at the largest. And I prayed for him to be correct, and the tumors would stop growing.

Chapter 5

Being boaters, all our time, energy, and money went to the boat. That is also where we spent all our vacation time because there was not any other money to take a formal vacation. As most are aware, having a boat and maintaining it in a saltwater environment is expensive.

I opened an online savings account to save for the annual boat slip fees. I also put tax return money and Christmas bonus money aside in this separate account and set up automatic transfers every pay week in anticipation of saving some money for a vacation outside of the marina. Paul was not a saver, and if he saw money, he wanted to spend it. The only way to start saving money is to start saving money, a little bit at a time. I did not hide the account, he knew it existed, he just did not know the balance or have the account information. If he had the money for the boat, he did not care about the rest.

The girls were ages eight and five, and I wanted to take them to Disney World. We had the summer slip already paid for, and there was money in the savings to pay for the vacation. I felt strongly with all our toys, that if we were going on a vacation, it needed to be paid for in cash so as not to add to our debt.

After meeting with Dr. U. and having to watchfully wait until the summer for additional scans, we decided to go to Disney in May. Paul was feeling well, had no pain, and looked as healthy as any other forty-four-year-old male. It made sense to go and make some family memories. Paul was completely on board with the plan.

May was the perfect month. It was after spring break and before their peak season, and temperatures were perfect. Paul loved to drive, and he really wanted to drive to Florida from New Jersey. After pricing out airfare and comparing it to the cost of fuel for the car round trip, it would be a difference of $1,000. We packed up the car with plenty of snacks and DVDs for the ride. We left early one evening, and Paul drove through the night, stopping every few hours to refuel and use the restroom. We arrived in Orlando within fourteen hours. He said he saw us all asleep and just drove. It was better I did not know how fast he had been driving for us to arrive two hours ahead of schedule.

We stayed at Port Orleans Riverside, and loved it. For Paul to make mention of how pretty and peaceful of a resort this was, it had to be ultra-impressive! He rarely gave high praise, relying more on pessimistic comments, but in his words, he "was impressed."

Even though he was looking and feeling well, he would get fatigued. The fatigue being the only symptom he had since his diagnosis and surgery. Between that and Kaylee being five, I planned afternoon downtime for naps for us all.

We did not attempt to do all the parks during this first trip but wanted to spend a lot of time in Magic Kingdom to feel like we really saw it all. We would eat a quick breakfast from the granola bars and cereal I packed and head to the park at opening and stay a few hours. At these ages, the kids were really interested more in swimming than being in the parks. We would have lunch, swim for an hour, and then nap. We would then head back to the park for the evening. This worked well for us, and we avoided cranky, overtired children and adults.

We visited Epcot to attend a princess luncheon. I had not planned on going to Epcot this first time, but since I planned this trip quickly, I had to take what I could get for times and places for character meals. The kids were not impressed with Epcot and wanted to go back to the pool. I was thoroughly enjoying Epcot—more than I thought I would—and would have liked to stay longer. But we headed back to swim and nap.

We lived in the moment and had a great time. Before booking the trip, I asked a lot of questions of people and patients I know who were Disney fanatics. I listened, took notes, and bought a traveling guide to Disney and utilized all their tips and advice, which only added to our enjoyment.

Traveling in the off-peak season made the hotel less expensive. We had no hard-set itinerary and just went where we wanted when we wanted. We did not rush and had no plans on doing all the parks in one week. Naps were the only thing scheduled, and it helped tremendously as we were not exhausted at any time during the week. The only thing we were not able to do was see Elsa and Anna for autographs as that was shortly after the release of the *Frozen* movie. The line, even with being present early, exceeded two hours at any given time.

Driving there we saved money by avoiding airfare. We were able to pack as much as we wanted since I had a large SUV. We also packed a lot of snacks which saved us from buying breakfast most mornings. I went to a Disney store at our local mall and bought souvenirs ahead of time, including the autograph books and pens (thank you, Tracy, for that tip). As the kids and Paul went out of the hotel room, I would place a princess nightgown or stuffed animal on the bed, and the housekeeping staff would place the gifts on the freshly made beds (again, thank you, Tracy). This saved us a lot of money at the parks. Plus, the kids were so excited to see what the Disney fairy left for them in the hotel. Another friend suggested the photo package. She is a single mom and said if she did not have the photo package, she would not have been in any of the pictures with her daughter. She made absolute sense and so I purchased the picture package and took advantage of all photographers throughout the parks. We got some great pictures.

Amazingly enough, the trip was fully paid in cash, and I even had money left over to put back into the vacation savings plan! I prayed for safe traveling to and from Florida and while at the parks. I praised God for having the funds for the trip as well as the beautiful weather and fantastic memories made that week.

Chapter 6

Prior to our trip, our oldest daughter, Kiersten, was in second grade. She had been overhearing conversations between Paul and me regarding his cancer when we thought she was asleep. We lived in a ranch-style home, and her bedroom was right off the living room. It is possible that she just heard us unintentionally and was not eavesdropping. Paul has always been loud, and his whisper would be considered normal volume, but she admitted to the eavesdropping at times.

She developed anxiety that would present itself during math lessons at school and would leave the classroom crying. She would go to Ms. W., the principal for some cuddling and praying and once calmed, returned to class. It was probably a nice break for Ms. W. from the usual administrative and disciplinary actions to hold a little girl on her lap, but it became a daily occurrence and was disruptive to the class, and Kiersten was missing part of the math lesson.

Her teacher, Mrs. G., came up with a plan. She placed Kiersten's desk against the side of her own desk and created a short slide show on her computer for her to view if she felt anxious. This slideshow included short verses about God, and several pictures of puppies (as she was and still is all about her dogs). It worked wonderfully and Kiersten was able to stay in the classroom. Then things escalated, and Kiersten hit her friend in the face one day. She had been "hearing voices" when her friends talked to her. It would be the voice of her friend, but the words would be changed to "You are stupid," or "You are dumb," and that day she had reached her limit. Kiersten was suspended from school for the incident and entered counseling.

The "voices" became a little scarier in what they were saying, and I called around to get her into a child psychiatrist. I spent two full days calling child psychiatry offices within a fifty-mile radius who took our insurance. All the scheduling screeners said the same thing, she needs help as soon as possible, but our next appointment is six, seven, or sometimes eight months out. I then looked up child psychiatrists in Pennington and Princeton to see what fees they charged, as none of them took insurance. It is interesting and disconcerting to see how many are available in these areas and the fees they charge are ridiculous, but they get it.

I got her an appointment five days later at $600 for a ninety-minute evaluation, and $200 for the thirty-minute follow-up session that occurred two weeks later. This follow-up was to review psychology forms that I filled out, as well as her teacher regarding hyperactivity disorder. I was reassured that my daughter was not schizophrenic in hearing voices but rather had some hyperactivity, combined with an immature seven-/eight-year-old brain who did not understand, and therefore could not process, some of the things she was hearing. It was money well spent for the relief of knowing she was okay. I had prayed for a simple explanation and hoped she did not have some serious psychiatric disorder. These were answered prayers.

Chapter 7

When we returned home from Disney, Paul made his appointment for his next set of scans which were done early June. We anxiously awaited the results, and I prayed for stabilization of the cancer. His tumors not only grew, one of them was now over three centimeters, and there were eight tumors now. Oh, and the tumor on the left adrenal gland looked to be cancer too. Surgery was needed and was scheduled for the next month. There had been a recent cancelation, otherwise, he might not have been able to be scheduled for many more weeks. Dr. U. stated that he was surprised at how rapidly the tumors grew. We were upset and disappointed at the news but not surprised. Something about this cancer seemed more ominous than other cases, and we continued to have feelings of something is not right.

The aim of this next surgery was to remove the tumors and spare the left kidney (otherwise, he would need dialysis) and remove the adrenal gland. We went to Fox Chase the morning of the surgery July 16, 2014. Despite the tumors, his kidney was still working excellently. And I prayed for a safe surgical experience, wisdom for Dr. U. and the care team, and a good outcome. Some, but not all, these prayers were answered.

When Dr. U. opened the abdomen, he did an ultrasound directly on the kidney to evaluate the depth of the tumors. Some were very deep and invaded the inner structures of the kidney and would cause a lot of damage if he tried to remove them. He started to count them (eight showed up on the scans), but he stopped counting at twenty. He decided to remove what he could while still sparing the kidney, as dialysis would have made his prognosis worse. He removed fourteen tumors, in total, and the adrenal gland, and all were positive for renal cell carcinoma. Dr. U. felt he had "reset the clock" on the cancer by removing as many tumors as he could, especially the larger tumors. We were not convinced and did not understand how anyone "resets the clock" on cancer. I did not think too much on it, and in hindsight, think that maybe he was just trying to offer us some hope, but he did not tell us anything of Paul's prognosis.

As I waited to be able to see him in his room, I called family members trying to explain it all. I was shaken and sat in the waiting room, physically shaking. I was shocked and stunned but that does not even begin to describe the sense of dread that sat in my stomach. My faith was surely being tested, and I had my moments of "Why, God?"

He stayed at Fox Chase for five days and recovered amazingly well. He FaceTimed with the girls as he did not want them coming to the hospital. They seemed to handle it well and spent a lot of time with their cousins as I traveled back and forth to Philadelphia. The nursing care, while not terrible, was not on par with HUP. His room was at the far end of the hall, and he had to get up, by himself, to search out his nurse to get pain meds after his epidural was removed. Fortunately, he did not hurt himself or fall in his efforts to get some help as his call bell was not being answered. I made sure that the nurse assigned to him was aware of this once I arrived and that I found their lack of response unacceptable. This can be a tricky situation as once a family member expresses displeasure in the hospital, it sometimes backfires on the care the patient receives. Some nurses and nursing staff will tend to avoid that patient's room when family visits to avoid any further conflict, and the family member gets labeled as "difficult." I had to word my complaint carefully and respectfully so as not to cause too many ruffled feathers. We had no further issues with the nursing care for the remainder of his stay.

While at Fox Chase, Pastor Emmons came to visit him again. Paul had showed up to church services with me twice after his first surgery, I think more as an obligation or way to say thank-you to

Pastor Emmons. He was certainly not a believer in Jesus, but he was asking a lot of questions, and I was sharing the gospel with him, or at least trying to share it with him as best as I could. During this visit, Paul asked pastor a lot of hard questions, but pastor was able to calmly and effectively answer his questions. Paul was attentive despite being medicated on morphine at the time. He was ready to listen after being told of the surgery findings. Paul came to accept Jesus Christ on July 18, 2014, while in that hospital bed at Fox Chase.

It was a huge turning point for us. He became supportive and engaged with the girl's school. He also started to attend church services regularly with me and the girls. I had prayed for healing before this. And I had prayed for his salvation and for him to find mental peace. While we did not get healing, he got salvation, and he was on the path to finding some mental peace.

When he got discharged from Fox Chase, we called his oncologist at HUP. We were told to make an appointment for three months later. We both said, "Yeah, I do not think so." We had taken the conservative approach, and it was not getting us far. His prognosis had changed for the worse, and it was time to take a more aggressive treatment approach.

He wanted to go to MD Anderson in Texas. I told him that Sloan Kettering is in NY, just one state away, as opposed to more than halfway across the country. We could drive to one but would have to fly to the other. Either way, he needed to heal first as he was just home from another major surgery. He did some research about the kidney cancer experts at both places and called Sloan to get an appointment. First, he needed to get the records from Fox Chase to forward them to Sloan.

We found out through reading his records that he was now at stage 4 with metastasis and a 0% chance of survival at five years. We were not told any of this, not even at his post-operative appointment. I am not sure who was to be delegated to break the news to us about the change in his cancer status, but it certainly did not come from the surgeon. I am angry about it now but too stunned then to do or say anything. We were just trying to put one foot in front of the other and get a second opinion for treatment.

Some people asked why not remove the kidney and get a transplant. First, people wait for years to get a transplant. Second, to get one as a cancer patient, you must be cancer-free for several years because the anti-rejection meds lower your immune system and that would allow any cancer in the body to grow unchecked. Third, as Dr. U. recorded in his operative note, sparing the kidney was better than removing it totally, as dialysis would have hastened his death due to how hard lack of kidney function is on the body overall.

The adrenal gland that was removed was found to have metastatic cancer from the kidney. This we knew after surgery due to the pathologist looking at it immediately. We did not know until we did our own research that Paul's cancer staging just went from a 2b to a stage 4 with mets (short for metastatic) with a life expectancy of fifteen months. That life expectancy would have been even shorter if Paul had needed dialysis.

As I stated earlier, after finding out the cell type of cancer, he was able to narrow his research efforts to be focused on what applied to him. He was quite impressive with what he found and how quickly he learned the medical terminology. He then started to listen to various lectures that had been done on the topic. MD Anderson puts on two different kidney cancer lecture series annually, one geared toward healthcare providers and the other geared toward patients and their families. What struck us with all the lectures he viewed was that none of the presented cases looked like his cancer. They all seemed to be similar in their presentation and treatment. Even though the statistics were rather dismal for survival rates, the patient cases presented responded well to their treatment plan. Nothing that I found in my online medical resources matched his presentation either.

I clearly remember him listening to one of the lectures, but at the time I did not know it was the lecture geared toward patients. I just half-listened and realized it was a medical conference that was "dumbed-down" in language. One of the presenting physicians from MD Anderson then went on to say that all kidney cancer patients will die of their disease within five years. Well, that got my attention but not in a good way. I was dumbfounded that a presenting physician would be so callous as to make such a blanket statement to a roomful of kidney cancer patients or their loved ones. I made Paul turn it off as hearing something like that, whether true or not, takes away a person's hope and can leave them despondent. He needed to have as much fight in him as possible if he was going to have any chance of survival.

Paul sent all his medical records and made the phone calls to Sloan Kettering. He wanted to do it, and I think he needed to do it. It gave him some control over the situation and kept him busy. He became very educated very quickly on advanced kidney cancer. Then we got the phone call from the Sloan scheduling department telling us that Doctor "A" (he was the top kidney cancer doctor there, but I do not remember or care what his name is) would not see him as he did not have significant enough disease. We were stunned and left baffled as to what did qualify as significant disease beyond stage 4 with metastasis at forty-four years of age? Seeing this strong and proud man with tears in his eyes asking me why and how a cancer patient can be denied an appointment left me shaken as well. I had no answer for him because I could not understand it either. He called the scheduling center back to try to get in with Doctor "B" or "C" but never received a call back. Clearly, Sloan Kettering was not where we were supposed to be. And if they called us back at that time to set up an appointment, we both would have had some very non-Christian words for them.

He then called MD Anderson and got an appointment with Dr. S. The process was repeated with sending medical records to them. After making childcare and doggie-care arrangements, we were on a plane two weeks later to Texas, in an August heat wave, to see their top renal oncologist.

And I prayed for his healing. I prayed for peace and understanding. I prayed for answers and an effective treatment plan and safe travel to and from.

Chapter 8

We had an uneventful flight to Texas and checked into our hotel which was a few blocks from MD Anderson. It was 110 degrees with a 100% humidity. It was awful. The entire health community in Houston is extremely impressive, but the sheer size of MD Anderson, along with their reputation, dwarfed it all. We ended up going across the street from the hotel to a small diner/deli that was attached to one of the medical buildings, clearly catering to the health staff. We both ordered burgers and fries, and Paul was the first to take a bite. He stopped mid-chew and looked at me and indicated that I needed to taste mine. I was hesitant, thinking something was wrong with the burger. However, this burger was the best burger ever! Paul swore that they must have just butchered the cow out behind the diner for the meat, it was so good. We could not get over how good it was.

We thought it had to be an anomaly. The next evening, we walked about a mile in the other direction and found another diner in a small strip mall and ordered the same. The conclusion, the same, best burger ever. We agreed we would travel back to Texas just to have a burger. I still smile at this memory. I have yet to have a hamburger that compares to these while in Texas.

We met with Dr. S., the renal oncology specialist. We arrived at the medical center well ahead of schedule as Paul just wanted to be there, regardless of how early we were. I highly doubted he would be seen earlier as people do not miss appointments at these facilities except for extreme emergencies. But it calmed his anxiety to just be there. We waited around for several hours, and felt it was worth the wait. The physician had reviewed his records ahead of the appointment and felt that he should not wait to start any type of therapy. It had been a month since the surgery, and it was okay to go ahead with treatment. He had an aggressive cancer but because he was young and healthy, he could handle being treated aggressively. She suggested returning to Fox Chase to see a newer kidney oncologist who had done her fellowship at MD Anderson and "was the best fellow I ever trained." She felt that getting care at a cancer-dedicated center would be better than staying at HUP, which has interests across many different disciplines. She would send a consult letter to the oncology doctor at HUP, telling her of her opinion. She was confident, but not cocky, that whatever she suggested would be done, as providers listen to what MD Anderson's physicians instruct them to do.

We had a plan and decided we would meet with this doctor at Fox Chase since they already had his records. While we liked the oncologist at HUP, and she had been at Fox Chase for years before going to HUP, we felt we needed someone more aggressive on our team. She did call us after receiving the letter from MD Anderson and offered us an earlier appointment than the three months originally stated. We declined and told her where we were going. She was polite and apologetic and wished us the best.

We met Dr. P. two weeks later at Fox Chase and immediately liked her personality, her demeanor, and her approach to Paul's situation. Many kidney cancer drugs cannot be started immediately after surgery as they impair the body's ability to heal. Paul was now six weeks post-surgery but needed to get scanned again to be re-staged. He wanted to participate in a new clinical trial that was a head-to-head comparison of a current therapy (sunitinib) versus a new immunologic combination ipi/nivo (short for ipilimumab and nivolumab) that had recently gotten approval for melanoma and was now being studied for kidney cancer. We prayed that he qualified, and if he did qualify, that he got the newer drug arm. He knew that the current medications for kidney cancer slowed down tumor growth for a few months before needing another plan. He really hoped the newer drug would give him a better outcome for a longer period of time. They all had their long list of side effects, but he was looking for something that would give him a longer range of time before needing to switch to another therapy.

Repeat scans on September 18, 2014, showed the remaining left kidney tumors, the largest measuring 1.7 cm. His lung scan showed some scattered nodules felt to be harmless as they had been present before, but not commented on, but there was polyp in the gallbladder, which was new. This would become important later. His brain scan was clear. There was a positive finding in the right hip muscle measuring almost 4 cm and was felt to be part of his cancer. There was no way to biopsy this mass to confirm it because of how deep it penetrated the muscle. It was not causing him any discomfort and did not affect his range of motion in his hip. This "metastatic" mass qualified him for study and gave us another answered prayer.

He signed all the forms and had all the required testing on his heart done along with a ton of blood work. He started the infusions and tolerated them superbly. He went every two weeks for the treatments with bloodwork every time. Since he had no side effects, he was able to drive himself to and from the hospital, so I did not have to take additional time off from work. His work schedule was super flexible and not an issue, and he wanted to continue to work. He was eligible to go out on disability, but he declined. He needed the distraction and to stay busy.

He had to have scans repeated to check for changes six weeks into the study and then every three months. And I prayed before getting the scan results for some good news, and we got some. The initial six-week scans showed no significant changes in the already mentioned tumors and no new tumors! We were thrilled and entered the holiday season with newfound optimism. The New Year would bring new changes.

Chapter 9

Surprisingly, despite having one kidney—and that one with tumors and parts of it removed—his kidney function was still normal. All his lab work remained normal. He looked great, his weight was stable, and he was tolerating the ipi/nivo infusions well. He still had fatigue but continued to work and would nap in the afternoons. He always napped, due to his depression, but now he napped due to fatigue. He continued his weekly therapy sessions with Tina. He got new scans done January 20, 2015. Again, we prayed for healing and continued stability of the cancer. We were thankful that he still looked and felt well and tolerated the cancer drugs well.

The chest showed new findings, not defined as cancer but as "ground glass and patchy densities that could be inflammation from the ipi/nivo infusions or infection [like tuberculosis]." He needed a recheck in three weeks. Inflammation is a big side effect of this drug combination and something the oncologist was monitoring for. He was able to continue the medication because he had no side effects. There was also new lymph nodes on both sides of his chest, measuring 1.9 cm. The left kidney tumors were slightly larger, as was the gallbladder polyp. The right hip lesion had not changed at all, and due to this, the radiologist now suggested that it was a synovial cyst and not cancer-related. It was good news that it was not cancer, but the fact that they initially thought it had been cancer qualified him for this trial.

Three weeks later, more bloodwork and scans. The bloodwork showed a slight decrease in his kidney function. This prompted a change in his mood-stabilizing medication by his psychiatric nurse practitioner. His current antidepressant/mood stabilizer could further damage the kidney. The change in kidney function could also make the blood levels of his medication go too high.

The chest scan showed a worsening of his lung findings overall and some fluid buildup in the lung. He had an oxygen level of 100% (I checked it at home) and no cough, no shortness of breath. That was amazing considering the results. The oncologist called us with the results and had arranged for Paul to see a pulmonologist the next day. He would need to have a bronchoscopy and biopsy done. The pulmonologist was optimistic that this was all inflammation from the cancer treatment. And we prayed that he was right. He was wrong.

February 2015, the bronchoscopy was done. It did not reflect anything specific from the lung washing and tissue samples. The doctor did, however, take a sample from the enlarged lymph nodes in his chest—now three of them—and they were all positive for cancer.

One month later, March 13, 2015, he had another round of scans done. He had been taken off the ipi/nivo trial when the bronchoscopy results came back positive for spread of disease into the chest lymph nodes. The chest scan now showed a clearing of the "ground glass densities," but was replaced by several prominent nodules, all appearing to be cancer. The chest lymph nodes were unchanged. His kidney tumors had enlarged slightly. Remember that gallbladder polyp from over a year ago? It had rapidly enlarged and was now being called a possible cancer, whether related to the kidney cancer or an entirely separate cancer had to be determined.

I did not accompany Paul on this visit. He felt fine and wanted to go by himself. Paul had become so well-versed in the treatment modalities and how each drug classification targeted different types of cells that he could handle going by himself for some visits, if necessary. It was nice seeing his confidence in his ability to navigate the hospital system and the medical understanding he had acquired.

I regretted it. I felt like a fool not going with him. Especially when I saw the office visit notes stating that "the patient presents to the clinic today alone." Dr. P. had planned, ahead of his appointment, for Paul to be seen by a surgeon to evaluate the gallbladder.

She had called us the night before when the last scan results were bad and he needed the pulmonologist, but she did not call us this time; otherwise, I would have been with him for both appointments. Paul put me on speaker to hear the conversation.

Dr. F., the surgical oncologist felt this was more likely a second cancer of the gallbladder and not part of his clear cell kidney cancer as there had not been any other cases of metastasis of kidney cancer to the gallbladder that he knew about. Nothing else about Paul's cancer seemed normal so why would this be any different? I felt this would be the first case this doctor has ever seen, and Paul would be written up in a journal as a case study. I did not know how to pray or what to pray that night. What was the lesser of the two scenarios—mets to the gallbladder or a second primary cancer of the gallbladder? Neither was good, but I felt having a second type of cancer was worse. At least if it was part of his kidney cancer, it was then all the same type of cancer. And I prayed for whatever God felt aligned with his plan. I had no words and felt numb.

The gallbladder tumor was metastatic clear cell carcinoma from the kidney. The surgery was performed laparoscopically but with difficulty due to scar tissue from his previous kidney surgeries. He stayed two days at Fox Chase with some minor difficulties related to bladder spasms and inability to urinate. Neither of us was too pleased with the nursing care provided, or not provided, on this stay. Paul called me several times the first night due to some issues. They got addressed, but it took the nurse longer than expected to address the problem. I made my presence known early the next morning once I got the girls to school and stayed as long as I could into the evening, making arrangements for family to care for the kids and dogs that evening. Fortunately, I was able to bring him home with me.

Chapter 10

Paul had more scans done at the end of April. More bad news. He had "too numerous to count" tumors through all lung fields. His lungs looked as if someone had blown talcum powder onto them, a bunch of little white spots everywhere. There was a new lesion just above his right diaphragm as well as in his peritoneum (stomach cavity lining) and into the liver. Despite these findings, he still felt fine. To me, the scans looked like "dead man walking" and did not match his physical presentation. He still looked healthy, was still working, and doing everything he had always done. No one would believe something was seriously wrong with him. I questioned, several times, if the patient's name was correct and if we were looking at someone else's films. Dr. P. chuckled at this as she said she was wondering the same thing but knew the scans were his.

He was taken off his clinical trial of the ipi/nivo when he had the positive lymph nodes. He was not eligible for any other trials currently being conducted, and he needed time for the drugs to come out of his system—a wash-out period—before starting any other medications. Paul checked the government clinical trial website (clinical-trial.gov) daily, looking for anything that he would qualify for, but at this time, there was nothing new posted. It was time for him to start sunitinib (sutent), one of the first kidney cancer medications to be released and first line treatment. It came with a wide range of side effects, and it was a sure bet he would be feeling these side effects.

Chapter 11

Since he was still feeling well, we had discussed going back to Disney again. I had enough money saved for the trip, and we wanted to visit the parks we did not go to on the first trip. We had planned the trip to go the week leading up to Memorial Day. It was God's grace that Paul was feeling well and had not yet started the new medication. It was as best a time to go as ever; the coincidence of the timing was not of our own. And I prayed for his healing still despite the odds. Our God is greater than we can imagine, and He could make it happen. I just was not sure why He would choose to do so and why He would choose us over someone else. I had to check myself, if I did not believe it could happen and did not pray in belief, then surely it is not going to happen. I prayed faithfully, and there were many prayer chains that included Paul in their prayers, but I still had moments of doubt and at times my faith ran low. I just never let it show.

Somewhere around this time, Mark Hall, a youth pastor and lead singer of my favorite Christian band, Casting Crowns, announced he was diagnosed with kidney cancer and would undergo surgery to remove his kidney. I told Paul this news, and after a few minutes, he said, "If that man has the same cancer and he is a youth pastor, then this cancer is not a punishment for being a sinful person; it just happens." Whether his reasoning was biblically wrong or right, it gave him comfort to think that God was not singling him out for punishment. Mark Hall also wrote a song titled "Oh My Soul" based on Psalm 43:5 that reflected his emotions at the time he got his diagnosis. A line from that song, "No one will see if you stop believing," resonated with my current feelings, and it is still a favorite of mine today.

Again, we compared prices of airfare versus fuel for the trip. I still had my large Acadia/SUV. We opted to drive again, or rather, Paul opted to drive again. He really likes to drive, especially long drives at night when he can go fast, and there is less traffic. We left early evening just before 5:00 p.m., about one hour ahead of schedule. We arrived in Florida around 6:00 a.m.!

Paul, despite the worsening of his disease, continued to look and feel remarkably well, except for the fatigue and some weight loss. We had beautiful weather which turned hot rather quickly the last two days of our visit. Again, we made the trip in May, but it was the last week of May instead of early in the month. We had a fantastic time and visited the parks we had not done the first trip, but this time we stayed at the Caribbean Beach resort. A quite different vibe from the Port Orleans Riverside and not as pretty, in my opinion. The rooms were the same, and the service the same; the pool, fantastic. But, if given the choice, I would choose to go back to Port Orleans Riverside. We only did Magic Kingdom one day, but we raced for the Elsa/Anna meet-and-greet at rope drop. We still waited thirty to forty minutes minutes, but it was so much better than a more than two-hour wait like the last trip. The kids got their pictures with the princesses and their autographs.

My favorite memory of the trip was an impromptu character breakfast at the Grand Floridian. It involved the Mad Hatter. Kaylee embarrassed Kiersten by telling this person that her big sister hit her in the mouth, on accident, with her big toe and knocked her loose, front tooth out. The man playing this character took this information and ran with it. I do not remember exactly what he said, but I remember we laughed until our sides hurt. Kiersten is not so much a fan of this story and rolls her eyes if it is mentioned.

I did the same thing as the first trip in packing lots of snacks and quick breakfast foods. Since we drove, we were able to leave Disney property, like we did the first time, and explore restaurants on International Drive for meals. I again stocked up on souvenirs from the Disney store and left gifts on the bed for the girls each morning.

We again bought the photo package. This time we did two Disney water parks.

We also had a dinner reservation for the luau at the Polynesian resort. Kaylee had fallen into a hard sleep that afternoon, and it was difficult waking her. She was grumpy. At dinner, she would not eat the chicken saying she was "not eating a cooked animal." Not sure where this came from as we are not a vegetarian family. It was amusing to us. She did participate in the show when they called the kids up onstage; however, she just stood there with arms crossed while Kiersten was dancing around. I chuckle when we look at those pictures. And I had prayed for safe travels and a good vacation with lots of memories. God answered all these prayers.

Chapter 12

Paul needed more scans done before he could start the new medication. His June 10, 2015, scans showed no new changes in the lungs (he had some improvement in the lung scans) or liver. The kidney tumors continued to grow. His films looked like there was more surface area of tumor than there was kidney, but it continued to function better than expected despite this. He started the new meds, and as expected, the side effects started too.

He had medication to counteract diarrhea and nausea and new medications to control an increase in blood pressure. He would have occasional mouth sores and pain in his hands and feet. While it made walking difficult, he never complained. He would need medications to help reduce his potassium levels as his kidney function was starting to fluctuate a bit but still in a good range, all things considered. We would shortly be taking a few trips to the emergency department.

Sometime during this period, Paul suggested I return to school to work on my doctor of nursing degree. He knew I was interested in this as I loved school, but I would never have fathomed returning to school with his future so uncertain. He argued that I should go back while he was still around to help me. He was also thinking ahead. I had myself in an ENT (ears, nose, and throat, or otolaryngology) specialty practice and had no intentions of going back into primary care. I needed something extra to help me when my current boss decided to retire in the future. He convinced me. I started researching schools and decided to enroll at Capella University as the program was online, accredited, was a bit less expensive than other programs, and they offered a $5,000 sign-on scholarship. Classes were ten weeks long, and I started my first class in July 2015. It turned out to be a good distraction from the curve balls life was throwing at us. I also liked to think that it set a good example for the girls as we would all be at the kitchen table doing homework together.

Chapter 13

During this time Paul's mom was having increased difficulty swallowing. She felt as if something was preventing her from being able to swallow solids. Mom Schroeder had been a heavy smoker for the past fifty plus years, with frequent—sometimes daily—intake of alcohol. She has never been a complainer, so if she complains of something, it really had to be bothering her. She got uncomfortable enough that she complained to her primary care provider and was sent for an x-ray. It showed a mass in the center of her chest which was compressing the esophagus, hence her difficulty in and sometimes painful swallowing.

I set her up with a local thoracic surgeon, Dr. L. I knew him from his surgical residency years at Hahnemann. He was excellent as a resident and had a very calm demeanor and wonderful bedside manner, and he happened to be at our local hospital.

Mom Schroeder was to be admitted for a mediastinal biopsy (taking a sample of the tissue from the mass in the center of her chest). This would require general anesthesia and therefore a breathing tube. What we did not know was that she had advanced COPD (chronic obstructive pulmonary disorder) from her years of smoking and had been "just chugging along." The anesthesia and high doses of oxygen delivered during the procedure changed all that. COPD patients live at lower levels of oxygen in their bloodstream due to the inability to properly exchange oxygen and carbon dioxide, because of smoking. When given too much oxygen, it affects their respiratory system in the brain and to counterbalance their altered gas exchange—they stop breathing. We could not get her off the ventilator. During one of the several attempts, over a few days, it caused too much stress on her heart and sent her into an irregular heart rhythm, atrial fibrillation. One thing led to another, and she was spiraling downward quickly as one body system after another became affected, like a domino effect. As a family, it was decided to insert a feeding tube and a tracheostomy. We know it was not what she would have wanted, but we hoped to stabilize her situation and get this turned around, making both tubes temporary, but it was bad. In the back of my and my sister-in-law Lori's—who is also a nurse—minds, we were skating a fine line of life and death and would not have been surprised it she did not recover.

Her biopsy results showed small cell lung cancer, the most common among smokers, but also aggressive. She needed to start treatment right away to shrink the tumor. While still unconscious, on a ventilator, she started chemotherapy. She lost her hair while still in the ICU, and eventually, with a lot of interaction with her lung doctor, she started to stabilize and got taken off the ventilator.

Paul, despite the many side effects of his medication, visited with his mom every evening. He would take scratch-off lottery tickets to her and read the results to her at the bedside. I instructed him on range of motion exercises to do on her arms and legs since she was immobile. During one of my visits, as her sedation medication was being lowered and she was able to move her extremities on her own, I realized her right leg was not as strong as the left side, and she was right-side dominant. We figured she must have had some type of neurological event, like a stroke, but could not prove it on brain scan.

The tumor responded well to the chemotherapy and was shrinking, relieving the compression on the esophagus. She was now awake and more stable but was still in the ICU, not walking, and still with breathing issues. Mom was not happy with her situation and one day mouthed to me that she wanted to die. But she pulled through. The tracheostomy tube and feeding tube were eventually removed. She was admitted to a rehabilitation facility for physical therapy. Unfortunately, she was able to make her own decision regarding her care at this time and opted for a facility that was not a high-level rehab, which is what I wanted for her and which was available for her. She spent longer than expected at this facility because the physical therapy was not intense enough to get her fully back to functioning and her right-sided weakness was not fully addressed. She did recover enough to come back home but never regained her pre-surgery health status or level of independent functioning.

During this entire process Pop Schroeder had to be cared for also. He was suffering with Alzheimer's and was more advanced than any of us realized. Mom did a good job of covering for him for several years, combined with a big dose of denial and no treatment being sought for his issue, he was too advanced for the normal medications to slow down the process. He had increasing anxiety and memory loss but was still able to function to care for himself to some extent and with some direction. He was still driving, for now. Peter and Patrick, Paul's brothers, took turns staying with their dad due to his high anxiety.

My attention and time were limited due to increasing issues with Paul's health. Peter, Paul's older brother, and Patrick, his younger brother, along with their significant others, Lori and Janet, took on the brunt of care of Mom and Dad. Peter especially took on a lot of additional responsibilities and became the go-to person.

During the preceding eighteen months of Paul's illness, we kept our families apprised of his status but also kept them at arm's length. Every family has their dysfunctions, and we just could not cope with any additional pressures being placed on us from personality differences, differing points of view, offering of advice, and any other reason. While I have been and still am close with my in-law family, Paul and I did not have a close relationship with my family, again due to varying reasons. I do not want to go into detail of the family dynamics as it is from my viewpoint only and could be hurtful. My mom and I have quite different versions of events that have occurred, so it is better to leave some things not written, as once out there, I cannot take them back.

My mom would try to placate me with words that "he will be okay, that poor man." I learned to save myself some frustration by ending the phone call. She clearly did not hear me or did not want to hear me when I would give her updates. Or I could just wait about thirty seconds and she would change the subject to something that concerned and centered on her. My sister, Kelly, would do the same thing. I tried to be graceful in thinking that they just did not know what to say as they had no experience in this area. But do not tell me it is going to be okay when I am telling you his cancer is getting worse and worse, every time we go for scans, every three months. He is going to die; he is not going to be okay.

Lori became my strongest warrior. She just got it and became my second backbone. Once Paul and I really allowed others into our circle with his disease, Lori was who we called on, time and again and again.

While Paul's mom was in the ICU and doing poorly, I had to take Paul to the emergency department. He would not stop vomiting despite the Zofran he was given for nausea and vomiting. We spent a long evening there. I would leave for a few minutes to go upstairs and check on mom and then back to the ER to sit with Paul. The ER tried various other remedies intravenously and finally Thorazine, an old antipsychotic medication sometimes used for severe vomiting, worked. He was able to be discharged a short time later. However, we would be returning shortly.

And I had prayed for mom Schroeder's healing, for her to wake up and breathe on her own, to talk to us and guide us again. And I prayed for Paul's vomiting to improve. We did not have a local oncologist for admission, but would soon if the vomiting continued, or we would have to go to Philadelphia for further care. Mom Schroeder did improve, and Paul did seem to get better from the vomiting issues.

Chapter 14

After a few hours' rest, I went back to the ICU the next morning. Lori met me there. I had been there for maybe thirty minutes when I got a text from Paul asking me to come home. I did not question it, just knew something was wrong, as did Lori, and headed home. If you remember the old Viagra commercials informing you to "seek medical attention right away if you experience an erection lasting longer than four hours" and thought it was a joke, it was not. Men joked about that warning talking about what they could do with an erection lasting longer than four hours and seeking emergency care was not on their agenda. As a former ER nurse, I have seen this happen. It is not a joke, it is an emergency, and sex is the furthest thing from a man's mind when this occurs. The man is in extreme amounts of pain, because it is not a normal erection, and nothing relieves it.

Paul had this unusual side effect from the medication used to stop his vomiting. It is called priapism. He had been experiencing this for the past few hours but did not want to say anything. Not sure why. He had been trying anything he could do to relieve the pain and engorgement without any success. He stated that he felt "funny" when leaving the ER after getting the medicine but was so relieved to have stopped vomiting that he did not worry much about it. Sex was not on his mind as he still felt awful and was exhausted so he could not figure out why he had an erection. Then it would not go away and was getting worse and more uncomfortable. He was now writhing in pain from it by the time I got home.

I took him back to the emergency room. Lori met me there. She works for the "sister" hospital and has connections. She was good at using those connections to make things happen faster. Few of the nursing staff knew what priapism was, or that it was truly an emergency or how it is treated. But the men in the department knew and acted quickly.

The ER physician was fabulous and completely empathetic. He had tears in his eyes hearing Paul's story. He said he was the same age and had young kids at home. He was envisioning himself in our position and all he could do was shake his head. He treated Paul with the utmost respect and compassion. The treatment sounds terrible but honestly, Paul did not care, he just wanted relief. After injecting an anesthetic into the side of the shaft of the penis, another needle and syringe are used to drain the excess blood, several syringes full, then a pressure wrap is applied so it does not refill with blood.

I made a call to his oncologist the next day to inform her of what had happened, and he was, of course, taken off the Sutent, and the Thorazine was made known as an allergy. He was now placed on another similar medication, same category medication, only a bit newer and maybe a few fewer side effects. This medication was called pazopanib, or Votrient. This was started at the end of August.

And I prayed that he would tolerate this medication and more, that it had the desired effect on halting progression of his disease for as long as possible. He did well on it. Much less stomach upset. He had some minor mouth sores and less foot/hand pain. He would continue this until November. His three-month scans showed that the tumors kept growing. He qualified for another drug trial but would need a fresh biopsy of the kidney tumors. Thankfully, this was done as an outpatient using an ultrasound guided needle biopsy. He was sore but no big incisions to heal from, so his recovery was quick. The biopsy did not reveal anything new regarding the cancer type or characteristics of the cells. Additional chromosome testing was done on the sample and revealed nothing unusual. We were hoping they would identify something to explain the aggressiveness of his cancer, but we got no additional answers.

Chapter 15

The new year, 2016, brought with it more new changes. We were exhausted being on a continuous emotional roller coaster, both working (he insisted on continuing to work) and maintaining as normal a routine as possible for the girls. They knew their dad was sick but did not really understand the enormity of what he was battling. Kiersten associated cancer with death as we had an English Mastiff, Susie, who died due to bone cancer, but she was not associating that with her dad yet. She believed God would heal him, and she had the beautiful faith of an innocent child. We all prayed for his healing, but it was becoming obvious that our will was not God's will.

He had new scans done in order to start the new drug trial. The scan results of January 13, 2016, revealed an overall worsening of all tumors and new ones in the chest, the abdomen, base of right pleura (bottom of lung lining), and pancreas. He was enrolled in a Fox Chase-based clinical trial combining immunotherapy of nivolumab (part of the first trial he was on) with interferon gamma injections every other day at home. The nivolumab was okay, he tolerated that well before, but the interferon gamma injection was some nasty stuff.

Paul was amazing. I was so impressed and proud of him. He had no hesitation in learning how to inject himself, and he wanted and was determined to do it himself. He only asked me once to give him his injection.

He would have to pre-medicate for some bad flulike side effects. He would be incapacitated for a few hours when the medication kicked in with high fevers and full body rigors (severe shaking). The side effects got progressively worse over the ensuing weeks.

On one of his treatment nights, Friday, February 12, 2016, Paul found me unconscious on the bathroom floor. I had not been feeling right all week. I honestly thought that with this last bit of bad news that I was on the verge of having a nervous breakdown. I was irritable and had no patience for anything, especially at work, treating patients who thought they were dying when they only had a sniffle.

I had been having headaches since graduate school, and they were getting worse. I got relief through massage therapy and exercise. I had been to my primary care provider several times who would always remark on how tight my neck muscles were. We both thought they were stress/tension type headaches as it was always a band around my head and a lot of pressure at the base of my skull. This same week, the headaches were worse and not responding to usual modalities. I felt a little bit dizzy on and off, and light hurt my eyes. I figured it was heading to a migraine, even though I did not have a history of migraines but would occasionally get a more severe headache that would abate over a few days. This Friday night, I skipped dinner due to some mild nausea. It was the height of flu and cold season. I thought I may have caught a stomach bug.

Paul injected himself and went to bed to try to sleep through some of the worse of the effects. He would be out of it for a few hours. The kids got tucked in for the night, and I went to bed early, but was up a short time later, in the bathroom pulling my hair back getting ready to vomit. Or so I thought. That was the last thing that I would be able to clearly recall for a few hours.

Kiersten heard something in the bathroom and saw me lying on the floor. She knew I was not feeling well and thought maybe I fell asleep there; she was only eight years old. She went back into her room and heard Paul get up. She thought, *He will see mom and know what to do.* He walked right past the bathroom, which still had the light on and the door open, due to his drug-induced stupor. He came back shortly after, according to Kiersten, and saw me on the floor. I had had a seizure and was unresponsive. He called 911, and then called Lori to come get the girls. Both arrived around the same time.

I had facial droop and was not talking, and while I could open my eyes, I did not focus on anything. He and Lori thought I had had a stroke. I do not recall any of it.

I do remember screaming when the EMS people took me out of the house due to the freezing temperatures. Then they got my attention again when they stuck a large bore IV in my arm. This was due to a hypersensitivity to stimuli because of whatever had caused the loss of consciousness, which turned out to be a seizure. In the ER, I had apparently regained enough consciousness to report that I had been nauseous. I was answering all the required questions correctly, though I recall none of it. They thought I was dehydrated and would give me IV fluids and discharge to home.

Paul was, meanwhile, sitting in the waiting room, looking terribly ill and shaking uncontrollably from his injection. The security staff for some reason kept blocking him from coming back. Lori worked at this hospital and arrived there as soon as she had dropped the girls off at her house.

She was annoyed at security. She had expected that a stroke alert would have been called and that a lot more done by the ER staff before she arrived. She immediately took control and got Paul into the ER to relay his findings to the ER physician. Then everything changed. A stat CAT scan of the brain was ordered. Lori had told them what I did for a living, and that if I were acting normally, I would be directing my own care. I remember just being exhausted and wanting to close eyes. My head hurt terribly, and the lights made it worse. I was coming out of my post-ictal state (what we call the period after a seizure before regaining full consciousness) enough to remember the ER doctor telling us that I had brain swelling from a brain tumor. I cried thinking we both cannot have cancer; we cannot leave our kids orphans. It made my head hurt even more. I could not think; I could not pray. I was helpless, as was Paul.

Once Lori told the nursing staff our situation, they wrapped Paul up in warm blankets and took pity on him. A short while later, Lori told me that they thought I had had a seizure. I quickly grabbed my crotch to check to see if I had wet myself, as most seizure patients lose control of bladder, and sometimes their bowels, during the event.

I had not soiled or wet myself, but it showed I was awake and able to connect the dots now, and as Lori said, "And she's back." My tongue was swollen and purple all the way around from biting it during the seizure and it was sore, and I could not talk properly. That was the least of my worries as the tongue heals quickly.

The neurosurgeon on call that weekend had a reputation that preceded him. He was excellent but also arrogant, as many tend to be in that profession. I felt comfortable staying locally as this surgeon was trained at Jefferson in Philadelphia and the nursing staff vouched for his excellence in outcomes. I had to rely on Lori's judgment and her knowledge about this surgeon. I trusted Lori and I trusted her opinion. If she said he was good, then he was good. She felt I was in excellent hands but wanted to make sure I was comfortable staying at the local trauma center.

With my heading pounding, I could not think well, but I remember rationalizing out our situation. Paul was ill. He could not take care of the kids and manage his treatment and try to see me in Philadelphia for however many days I would need to be there. I just needed someone to save my brain. Lori said Dr. V. was the best and her hospital had a brand-new neuro ICU (she knew most of the nurses there, too, and vouched for their expertise), so I opted to stay at her hospital.

The neurosurgical physician assistant came to see me. The neurosurgeon arrived sometime later to review the scans and complete the admitting orders. Dr. V. was a calm and reassuring presence. He explained that he did not think I had brain cancer, but rather a meningioma, which is benign (not cancer) and had probably been growing for a long time. It compressed the brain and pushed it over as far as it could go (7 mm), and it could not go any further, hence the seizure. People with traumatic brain injuries that have 8 mm or more of brain swelling do not survive.

I was started on pain meds to control the headache and high-dose steroids to stabilize the swelling as well as anti-seizure medications. I would undergo some MRI's that weekend in anticipation of having brain surgery on Monday. I slept, a lot. Apparently, there were many visitors through the weekend, my mom, our pastor, our friend,

Karen, and even my boss, but I do not recall much of it. The kids said they came to see me too.

I was admitted to the neuro-ICU and had wonderful nursing care. Lori checked on me often. That weekend is still foggy and the following ten days or so were an almost complete blank except for what has been filled in by Paul and Lori and reading my medical records.

Somehow, through sheer determination, I had a moment of clarity on Saturday and asked Paul to bring me my school laptop. He thought I was nuts. I had an assignment due on Monday and I had already finished it, just had not submitted it yet.

I needed to submit it and let school know I would not be participating in the classroom due to the brain surgery. I could not see clearly and had poor hand-eye coordination, but I managed to do it anyway. But the effort cost me. It made my head pound more despite the Percocet. The class instructor was very accommodating. We were halfway into this class, five of ten weeks. I was not able to participate in the online class discussions because I could not see well or concentrate on the screen, but I managed to finish the class anyway with a 4.0 due to many factors that worked in my favor.

And I know I prayed. I am sure I prayed for wisdom for Dr. V. and his team and for a full recovery, but I honestly do not remember. The surgery went as planned and went well. Paul brought the girls to visit, but they reported to me later that they were very scared and upset because I looked like an alien. The right side of my head and face was distorted and swollen and my right eye was swollen shut and purple. Dr. V. was gracious in that he trimmed the hair short where he needed to make the incision but did not shave my head.

Despite being very dizzy and not able to walk straight, blurry vision, and difficulty with hand-eye coordination, I was discharged home two days later as I passed the physical therapy evaluations. I had been working out five to six days a week before getting ready for work doing spin, step aerobics, interval training, and yoga. I got relief of the headaches, only temporarily, but it was still relief. I was in good shape and am amazed now that I was able to do any of it with a tumor in my brain.

I remember being pushed in a wheelchair to the pickup entrance, and I know that Paul drove me home, but I could not remember what vehicle he used to get me home. Paul now became my caregiver and meticulously adhered to the medication regimen of pain meds, seizure medications, and steroids that would decrease in dosage over the next few weeks. It was a role reversal. He was still taking the experimental medication injections and going to Fox Chase every two weeks for the infusion of the second part of the combination. He was amazing.

I would place several ice bags around my head to get pain relief and sleep. I did a lot of sleeping as is normal after brain surgery. The brain just cannot handle the stimuli, and it is lights out for several hours at a time.

One afternoon, I started screaming. I was still hypersensitive to touch, smells, and sounds especially. My head hurt, and I was hallucinating. Giant ladybugs were crawling on the ceiling and growing eyelashes to wink at me. I would see a flash of a bug crawl across Paul's leg, but was okay because I knew it was not real and it was not my leg. I can handle blood and guts, just not bugs.

Paul called the neurosurgeon and drove me to the ER in South Jersey where Dr. V. was currently working. He met us for another brain scan and lab work. I am not afraid of needles and needlesticks have never bothered me, but the hypersensitivity to touch amplified the needlesticks several times over. My scan showed improvement in the swelling of the brain, but I still had a long way to go. I was now at a 5mm brain shift, and my medication doses were too high. The medications got adjusted, and I was sent home. Despite the fatigue, headache, and dizziness, I did have moments of functioning and clarity, just not for long periods. I was one week after surgery.

The following week, I scooted down the basement steps (on my butt, as I was too dizzy to navigate steps) to get my disability insurance information. We had a partially finished basement, and I had a craft room/computer station on the other side of the laundry room. I was pleasantly surprised.

I had completely reorganized the basement the week before I had the seizure. I just did not remember that I had done so. I had reorganized and labeled all my filing drawers and cleared out the paper clutter. It was a really, good system. I easily found everything I needed to file my temporary disability claims through AFLAC.

I likened it to a pregnant woman who starts nesting in the third trimester, but I think it was God getting me prepared for all that was to happen in 2016. I honestly believe He was trying to tell me something, and I was not listening. I just kept busy and pushing my way through everything, so He knocked me flat on my butt in a big way. I had no choice but to pay attention and listen. I remember praying, "God do what you will to test my faith and Paul's new faith, but please do not allow harm to our girls." Images of Job being tried by the Satan by having his entire family wiped out flashed in my mind. I knew I would surely not withstand that trial if it were to occur. Thankfully, I was not tested in that way.

Chapter 16

I was not allowed to drive for the next six months due to the seizure and brain surgery. I knew I was not safe to drive anyway, and it was the least of my concerns. Paul was still doing his immunoglobulin gamma injections every other night and getting worse side effects. Besides the fevers and shaking, he was getting increased headaches, dizziness, and vomiting. All of which were listed as a possible side effect. He was getting worse and was really bad the night of March 11. He stayed in the living room to be closer to the kitchen sink to vomit so as not to wake me up. I would get up every few hours to refresh the ice bags and check on him, and he said he was okay, until I checked on him at 5:00 a.m. He told me he could not get up without falling, his head was going to explode, and he could not stop vomiting. He looked terrible, and I was helpless to do anything for him.

I called Lori and burst into tears when she answered. I cried, "We need help." I tried to explain to her what was going on and that Paul needed to go the hospital. I had no idea what to do about the kids and school. They were still sleeping. Paul was my priority right then, and I could not handle more than one thought and task at a time. She took control and said she was getting dressed and would be over in ten minutes. Peter would be over to help with the kids and school and drive me to the hospital. She called me about an hour later from the ER with the news that Paul's cancer had spread to the occipital part of his brain (the back of his head), and he had swelling around the tumor from the cancer drug which is why his symptoms were worsening during his injection days and he was better on the days off. Peter took the girls to school and then took me to the hospital.

He was admitted to the same neuro-ICU that I was in one month prior. The ER staff remembered us from my visit, and of course, so did the ICU staff. They were wonderfully kind. They took care of me with reclining chairs and blankets when I visited with Paul during his eight-day stay in the ICU as I was only four weeks from my surgery.

He, too, would need brain surgery to remove his cancer. He had brain surgery exactly one month after my brain surgery. While I had the larger brain tumor and swelling, his diagnosis was more severe, yet he would recover and be driving and back to work three weeks later. But his post-operative recovery in the hospital was not easy.

It was day 2 after his surgery and the neurosurgical ICU team had just evaluated Paul during the morning rounds. I had gotten a ride to the hospital by my mom after she dropped the girls off to school. Lori would be joining me shortly as she reported to work. Paul whispered to us, in as low a voice as he could, which was not low, that I needed to call the police because there was a "Mexican flop house here, and they were holding people hostage." He was serious. We found out that a Hispanic man had died during the night from a massive brain hemorrhage, and the family was large, loud, and hysterical in the hallway speaking in rapid Spanish. I groped my way down the hall to tell the ICU team what was happening.

They performed a more in-depth neurological exam. By this time, other family members were present, and Lori asked Paul to name us all. I was "wifey," then Patrick, Janet, and Lori. Lori asked him what my name was, and again, I was "wifey." Despite the seriousness of the situation, we were all quite amused by his story, and we still have no idea what a Mexican flop house is. He had a stat CAT scan done of his brain which revealed significant swelling to the area of his brain where the tumor was removed. He was potentially in grave danger if the swelling could not be stopped and reversed.

He was placed on a high-sodium infusion and given a diuretic that helps pull fluid from the brain. Think of someone lost at sea and drinking the salt water. He was parched, intentionally. His lips and mouth were caked and crusted and bleeding due to the dryness. They would not give him any pain medications, except for Tylenol, for the headache to be able to detect any subtle neurological changes. If this did not work, they were prepared (and already set up in the room) to make a burr hole in his skull and insert a drainage tube to drain the fluid from the brain. This, of course, has its own set of complications, namely, death from infection.

Paul would ask anyone who came into the room, "Do you have any water?" He was still confused; he could be oriented to why he was so thirsty and understand the theory behind it but would forget it two minutes later. One of the night nurses found him drinking the water from his melted ice bag he used for his headache. No more ice bags! After a few days, he was responding to the treatment and could drink Gatorade only, due to the salt content. A few more days, and he was declared much improved. He was oriented and allowed a regular diet and would be discharged home with a tapering dose of steroids and salt tablets. He still needed to limit water intake, so the swelling would not reoccur. Peter took care of bringing him home.

Paul was more clearheaded than I was, and except for head pain and some dizziness, was able to function fully. He was also able to manage both our medications post-surgery. Two weeks later, he had a follow-up visit with the neurosurgeon and was cleared to drive and return to work. His brain CAT scans were back to normal. He had no ill effects from the brain surgery at this time and was back to full functioning. Except his appetite. He never regained his full appetite and started to lose weight.

Chapter 17

Paul was, of course, taken off the trial as it was not controlling the cancer. We met with Dr. P. a few weeks after his brain surgery. Paul had additional scans done while in the hospital for the brain surgery which showed some new masses. These scans needed to be reviewed and a new plan developed. The scans showed new metastatic masses in the remaining right adrenal gland and was already measuring 1.7 cm × 1.5 cm; at the base of liver; on the left retroperitoneal area (back part of his left abdominal cavity), next to the psoas muscle; and in several new spots in his lungs as well as enlargement of several of the previous masses in his lungs. He also developed a small pleural effusion on the right side (fluid filling up between the lungs and lung lining) and some patchiness in the left base of his lungs suggesting inflammation or infection. Amazingly, he had no complaints of shortness of breath and his oxygen levels were 100%; all his blood work was normal. He had no complaints of any pain. And he still looked good, just a little bit thinner. Despite the scans, no one would even suspect he was this sick.

He would start cabo, short for Cabozantinib, next in line of the kidney cancer medications. He started this April 13, 2016. Two days later, we were back in the emergency room for chest pain and shortness of breath. My concern was a worsening of the pleural effusion, but all the emergency room physician cared about was making sure he did not have a clot in his lung, a pulmonary embolism. Cancer patients have an increased risk of having blood clots due to the metabolic effects that cancer has on the body.

I had heard a rubbing sound on the right side of his lungs when I listened with my stethoscope before going into the ER. While in the ER, not a nurse or the physician placed their stethoscope on his chest to listen to lung or heart sounds. The ER physician was lacking in communication skills and bedside manner. At the end of our visit, I made sure to let him know that I was not pleased with his lack of taking a history, lack of full assessment, and lack of listening ability. He did not care that he had a pleural effusion, only of ruling out the embolism. I was out of patience, frustrated, tired, and scared.

This was only two months after my brain surgery and one month after Paul's brain surgery. I cannot drive, I cannot walk straight, and I have a husband whose results keep getting worse. The ER physician could not give me any information regarding the pleural effusion—even though a CAT scan was just done—only that he did not have an embolism, his EKG was fine, and there was no explanation for his chest pain and shortness of breath. We were glad to leave and go home. We called Dr. P. to inform her of the ER visit and set up a follow-up visit. He was told to stop the cabo as maybe it was a side effect from it.

Between April and May of 2016, he started another medication, in the same line of the previous three, but next in line of being newer, called Lenvima or Lenvatinib. His lab work was starting to show abnormalities. His kidney function was a little worse, his overall metabolic profile was abnormal (electrolytes, liver function tests) but not grossly abnormal. He had mild anemia due to the kidney issues. His appetite was still down, his weight was down twenty pounds, but he was still up and functioning. While he was skinny at this time, little did I realize how skinny he would get later in our journey. He went to work every day, had no complaints of pain, and he was still fighting. At some time during this past year, his mantra became "never surrender." He had orange rubber bracelets made with his mantra on them and gave them out to anyone who wanted to wear one, orange being the color designated for kidney cancer awareness. I know I continued to pray, but my prayers were filled with silence. I did not even know what I needed. I gave it to Him. He knew what I needed, and I let him search my heart.

Chapter 18

The year prior, or maybe even a bit longer, Paul had started talking about his mortality. We both knew the statistics were against him surviving. He talked about not being around for so many big and small events in the lives of our girls. He wanted to plan an event where he walked them down the aisle and recorded father-daughter dances with each of them, when we felt the time was right. He talked about this at the marina and with his coworkers and our families. I had made mention of it to two friends at church who are great party planner/organizers for various events and happenings at church during the fall of 2015. They were ready to jump on it immediately and would have had it planned out that weekend. I told them I would let them know when we were ready to plan this event, a family celebration as I called it. May 2016, we decided it was time.

I called Jen and Renee and told them we were ready to plan this event, but I desperately needed their help. Renee called Pastor Emmons to clear it with him and check his availability as well as the availability of the church for June 4, 2016. We were good on both accounts. I told them this was to be a simple event, the focus being on Paul and our girls. We would serve appetizers and have the dances recorded and pictures taken. Recording the event was the most important. There were several photography people in our congregation, and Renee reached out to them but got no response. She and her daughter then called a videographer from NY who had done some work at one of the church events, but he wanted a full wedding video price for an event that I figured would take less than an hour from start to finish. We needed to figure out the photography and video parts first as they were the most important.

Paul decided to take matters in his own hands regarding the photographer and videographer and placed a call for help from friends on—what else—Facebook! A high school alumnus had a small business site that she posted our plight on, and the response was incredible. We had offers of exotic car rentals and photographers and an array of other stuff. We declined most of the offers as it would make this event much bigger and more complicated than what we wanted. We called one of the photographers, Racquel Marie Photography, who graciously offered her services free of charge. Another friend referred us to a videographer, Scarlett Creek Productions, who also offered services free of charge. Now that these two services were secured, we could figure out the rest of the budget and planning. If we ended up serving peanut butter and jelly sandwiches and lemonade afterward, I did not care—too much.

Paul's mom drove me to a children's clothing consignment shop, The Growing Place, that I frequented, to look for dresses. By this time, mom was doing well. She had gotten brain radiation to prevent her lung cancer from spreading to the brain, but it left her with some memory issues. Her hair was starting to grow back from her chemotherapy treatments. Her right side was still a bit weaker than the left side, and it showed in her ability to control her speed in the car, her walking, and her handwriting. But she was alive and functioning.

I was lucky that Renee, the owner of The Growing Place, had communion dresses still in stock even though we were past Mother's Day. She knew why I was there and left me and mom in the store on the pretense of going to the deli to pick up her lunch so we would not see her cry.

We found two dresses in the right sizes and styles that each of the girls would like. Renee told us to just take them, not accepting any money for them. She then asked how else she could help. I told her I needed to find someone for food, but something simple. It would be between lunch and dinner, so simple finger-type foods or an array of appetizers. She said she knew someone that might be able to help. She put me in touch with Sal, owner of Mannino's 3, who readily offered to cater our event. Cancer had touched his life, and he was so generous in the food he donated to our reception. We had more than enough food, and it was delicious.

The girls picked out their own shoes. Kaylee is a tomboy all the way. I really thought she would pick out plain flat shoes, and Kiersten would pick something fancy. I was wrong. It was totally opposite. Kiersten picked the plain white flats, and Kaylee picked out light pink heels with flowers. She said she liked the sound they made on the floors!

A friend from the marina, Karen, drove me to some flower shops. We picked out simple arrangements in mason jars. We also ordered a small bouquet and wrist corsages. Karen announced that she and her husband Jack were covering the flowers. My sister, Kelly, provided the cake and cupcakes.

Paul and I met with Pastor Emmons to discuss the ceremony. We all agreed that the act of walking the girls down the aisle would only take a few minutes, and we needed something more to make it a "ceremony." Paul had always wanted to renew our vows at the twenty-fifth anniversary year, but we were only at twenty-one years. He was not going to make it to the twenty-fifth. We decided to include a vow renewal and a family sand pouring ceremony. We would then come off the stage and I would sit. Paul would circle to the back of the church, and the girls would split up and circle around the outside perimeter of the pews to meet him at the back. He would then walk each daughter, individually, up the aisle.

We picked out the father-daughter dance songs. Kiersten picked "Cinderella" by Steven Curtis Chapman, a Christian artist, and Kaylee picked "My Little Girl" by Tim McGraw. We had to get permission for the dances from the elders of the church board as dancing was not allowed in the building. I was told by Pastor Emmons it was not a hard decision for anyone to make.

Now I had to find a dress. My mom took care of this one. She took me out to Macy's, and we found a perfect long, off-white dress. Not only was it on sale, but Mom had told the story to the store manager, who took an additional $50 off the dress. I think the dress and shoes combined cost just over $100.

Renee, from church, arranged for me and my girls to have pedicures, manicures, and our hair done the morning of the event. VC Salon did a fabulous job of our nails and simple hairstyles for the girls. My hair was a bit more difficult as the left side was very thin due to the cutting of the hair for the brain surgery. It was still long which helped the stylist pull and pin it up. As a final touch, they also did my make-up as there was an available artist.

Our family celebration, as I called it, took place on a lovely Saturday afternoon. All went as planned. The song "Yours, Mine, Ours" played as the girls and I walked down the aisle and again while we did the sand ceremony. The vow renewal was beautiful.

We stepped off the stage, and Paul walked to the back of the church. He walked down the aisle with Kiersten and then went back for Kaylee. We played Heartland's "I Loved Her First" for this. There was not a dry eye in the house. I had placed a wicker basket of packs of tissues at the vestibule entrance for our guests, knowing this was going to be very emotional.

We proceeded to the cafeteria/gym of the church known as the FLC or Family Life Center. Paul and I each gave a short speech, and I said a blessing for the day, the food, and our gathering. Then the father-daughter dances started.

Paul and Kiersten danced to "Cinderella." Everyone, men, and women, were dabbing at their eyes when this started, but the entire room started sobbing when Paul picked her up in his arms halfway through it. Occasionally, we hear it played on the Christian music station and it brings back bittersweet memories.

Kaylee was up next. She was concentrating so hard on her foot movements with Paul. It was so sweet. Then he picked her up too. It was hard to watch but beautiful too.

We decorated in the same colors as our original wedding, peach, and sea foam green. We also placed our wedding pictures around the perimeter. Jenn and Renee made sure everything was set up. They waited on the deliveries of food and flowers. They made sure the coffee, tea, and drinks were ready.

They were also the teardown committee, helping to load it all back up in the car, which took a few trips. Paul went home after the guests left, taking the girls and our personal mementos with him. My sister and I, despite my own fatigue, loaded the rest in her vehicle and took it home. We had a second trip to make to pick up the catering trays and return them to Sal. It was physically exhausting and emotionally exhausting, but we felt such relief and satisfaction at having this ceremony completed for the girls. And I prayed to thank God for the day and the generosity of everyone and for the love that was in that church.

At ages ten and seven, the girls were excited and had fun. They did not realize how momentous this event was or how important we hope it becomes to them when they are older. I had the pictures made into individual photo albums for the girls, and we have several copies of the video.

I had given permission to the photographer, Racquel, to post some of the pictures on her website. She then requested that I set up a GoFundMe page so she could link it with the pictures. This was something that I had not even contemplated doing. I put up a page with a fundraising goal of $1000 to go toward funeral costs. By the time I took the page down, March of 2017, we had almost $8,000.

Chapter 19

Two weeks after our ceremony, Paul got scanned again. The results were mixed. Some of his tumors were unchanged, some had responded to the medication and gotten a bit smaller, and there were a few new ones. He now had bone involvement along his right rib measuring 1.7 cm and another new one invading the muscles of his back, under his left shoulder blade. Both were giving him some discomfort. He continued the current medication and was sent for palliative radiation of the new lesions. Palliative means it is not a cure, just a treatment to help reduce his pain by shrinking the tumors, hopefully.

He continued to lose weight, another few pounds, as he had no appetite. He continued to work but at a reduced schedule. He went into the office every morning but would come home by lunch and sleep. He would spend the afternoon and evenings, off and on, working from home, answering his work phone to address contract and union employee concerns. He started to reduce the amount of travel he did to northern New Jersey for union business due to his fatigue.

And I prayed for relief of pain. I also prayed to slow the growth of these tumors. These tumors were popping up at a 1/2 inch in size within just a few weeks between the scans. My prayers were no longer for healing but for stabilization of the cancer. The two tumors responded well to the radiation and his pain, while not completely gone, was improved and manageable. I was doing much better myself. The brain swelling was gone; the headaches were gone. I still had some lightheadedness, but it was manageable. I was still not cleared to drive, but the seizure medication had me stable, and I was not having any seizure activity. I was exercising but not to the extent I had been. I could not tolerate more than twenty-five minutes of any activity; otherwise, I would be completely exhausted and dizzy for the next two hours. This occurred even with planting small flowers in the garden. We had hired a housekeeper, a friend, right after my surgery. She was a blessing to me and good company when she came over.

Chapter 20

I want to backtrack a bit to tell you about our years boating. We had a boat before we had wedding rings. We started out in the early '90s with a twenty-one-foot cuddy cabin Bayliner. We named the boat *Miss Guided*. The name stuck for the subsequent boats, and we just added in numeral numbers after it ending with our Tiara as *Miss Guided III*. A few years later, just before we got married, we upsized to a twenty-six-foot Sea Ray. Both were great boats. Paul was meticulous in the maintenance of them. Paul had never been on a boat until we started dating in high school. My parents owned a Bayliner with a large cabin. Paul was hooked on boating the moment he came aboard one afternoon. He immersed himself in all things boating. It became his obsession, and oftentimes, it took priority over other obligations.

After we took the New Jersey safe boating class together through a local chapter of the United States Power Squadron, he became an active member. He took all the classes they offered, started teaching the safe boating classes, and got a captain's license. Paul was excellent at anything he took an interest in and called himself a "jack of all trades, master of none." He was a great fixer of stuff and great at mechanical work. On weekends, he was always doing preventative maintenance on the boat or working on someone else's boat.

One summer, we planned out a boat trip from Barnegat to the Chesapeake Bay. We had our Sea Ray Sundancer and were traveling with another boating family who would meet us at the C&D canal, as they were coming out of the Delaware River. We had a fabulous week exploring several creeks. We had used a book called *Guide to Cruising the Chesapeake* to plan our stops. We docked in places that were within walking distance from the marinas to restock our supplies.

We had always done surf fishing on Island Beach State Park before getting a boat. Once Paul went fishing off a boat, there was no more surf fishing. He went offshore tuna fishing with a friend at the marina. He loved it and learned as much as he could. He had custom tuna rods made. He started making his own tuna lures. But we could not do this on our Sea Ray.

We started to look for another boat, one that met both of our needs—a cabin large enough for us and the dogs and allowed for serious fishing. We found the ideal boat in an older model thirty-one-foot Tiara Open. It had the perfect-sized cabin and a large open deck for fishing, plus a nice wide beam at twelve foot. It was solid and stable. It had the range for offshore fishing at the canyons but guzzled the fuel with its twin Chrysler big blocks. We purchased it in Maryland, and Paul and his friend Mike had an adventurous trip to bring it up the coast to Barnegat.

After two to three years, we made the decision to change the engines out for diesels. Paul did all the research and the layout to accommodate the diesels. Then we had to pay a "certified Cummins's mechanic" to install the engines and certify them. The mechanic was quite impressed with Paul's work as the engines slid right into place and no other adjustments were needed. The boat ran smooth, had more power, was faster, more economical to run. and had the offshore range he needed.

Many of our boating friends were happy to split the costs to go tuna fishing with Paul. Due to his fastidious care of the boat, they knew they would get back to land. They knew he had enough extra supplies to rebuild an engine at sea if needed. You just were not guaranteed to come back with fish.

We took two more trips to the Chesapeake on this boat, exploring different areas each time. We made a point to go back to St. Michaels, which became my favorite town and to dock on the Sassafras River. Both were favorites. This was all before we started our family. I still cherish the memories of these trips. They were fantastic, relaxing, well-planned, and a wonderful way of exploring the bay and coast of Maryland.

On our last trip, we went exploring up a river across from St. Michaels. We dropped anchor in a quiet, secluded cove. The water was warm and calm. The scenery beautiful with greenery along the shore. Birds were everywhere and the bugs were not too bad. We found our location on a chart and saw we were amid a bird sanctuary. It was spectacular. Fish were jumping out of the water and the birds were chirping, the water was calm and warm. The next morning, we went back to St. Michaels to refill our water tank and then headed back to our cove to anchor for another night.

A commercial crabber came along, and we got to watch how they worked their crab lines. It was so different than how we crabbed in Barnegat bay and fascinating to watch. Paul called them over and purchased a dozen blue claws for ten dollars. These crabs all measured between seven to eight inches point-to-point, which for that area was considered small- to medium-sized crabs. They were huge compared to our Barnegat crabs, and we were thrilled to get them. We cooked them that night along with a steak on our propane grill. It was delicious, filling, and memorable.

Paul loved his diesel engines so much that he designed a hoist and blocks for the engines to take them out during the winter. While he did not do it every winter, he did it often enough through the years that he could put them back into place and have them hooked up and running within an afternoon. This took winterizing your boat to a whole new level.

He took a lot of flak for this, and many jokes were made at his expense. But the men were impressed at the same time. In the garage, Paul would wrap the engines in cotton tarps. Before spring, he would touch up the white paint, inspect hoses, oil, and grease everything. The boat bilge would be degreased, and sometimes painted again, and so clean you could eat off it.

When the boat came out of the water in November 2015, Paul decided to take the engines out again. I was very hesitant about this. As his disease progressed, so did his fatigue. I did not know that 2016 would include brain surgeries for both us and worsening of his cancer, but I was worried he would not be able to put the engines back in the boat when spring came. He had no fears about it and took the engines out of the boat and into the garage.

Chapter 21

We had always dreamed about getting a small center console boat for playing around in the bay, water skiing, and tubing. We could never really afford the extra expense of owning two boats and having to pay for two boat slips. One was expensive enough.

In the early part of 2013, before Paul was diagnosed with cancer, he had sold the ATV he owned and used the money to buy a beautiful, new, center console, twenty-one-foot Robalo, with a light blue hull that we saw at a boat show. We had dreamed about having this type of boat for a long time. We looked at many center console boats at various boat shows and knew immediately upon seeing the setup on this boat that it was the one.

The money he got from the ATV put a nice down payment on the boat and made the payments manageable. The bigger boat had long ago been paid off, as was the loan for the diesel engines. We had so much fun on this boat for the few years we had it and the girls loved it too. It was perfect for quick excursions on the bay and taking the girls tubing. Plus, it was much easier to clean than the big boat. Somehow, we made it all fit into the budget for the additional marina slip fee.

Spring 2016 came, and the little boat was launched. The big boat was still on land as the engines were still in the garage. Paul really did not have the energy or stamina to put the engines back in but knew it needed to be done. Midway through the summer, he made it happen. We were getting to the point that he knew the time to sell the boats was getting closer, and we could not sell the Tiara without engines in it.

It took him a few hours longer to get it done, as he needed to rest often and nap, and he needed some additional help to do it. I prayed he would be able to accomplish it without getting hurt. My prayers were answered as the engines got installed, without incident, and they ran as smooth as always.

It was hard getting to the marina this summer. I was still not allowed to drive, and we both battled fatigue due to our respective health problems. Midway through the summer, I discovered that my neurologist never reported me to the DMV. I still had an active license, and my EEG (test for seizures) was normal. I was feeling better except for the fatigue. I started to drive again, but locally. I was nervous at first, but within two weeks, I was ready to drive to the marina like we used to do every weekend.

Our summer family vacation was a week of camping and boating at the shore. We packed up the camper and secured a spot at a local campground that had a large pool for the kids. It was near the marina and made for easy travel back and forth. It was a lot of work to pack up the camper for the week and then pack to go home and clean up once we got home. Paul slept for many hours through the day while I took the kids to the pool or rode bikes around the campground. I needed to still take a nap during the afternoon but a short one. The kids would watch a movie while the parents rested. We also brought the dogs along for the week, all three of them. We always had the dogs with us at the boatyard so bringing them with us in the camper for the week was normal but made for more work.

In hindsight, we should have arranged to leave the dogs home, but we were used to having them with us in the camper and at the marina.

During the camping trip Paul slept, often, but he tried to be present and do some activities with us, as much as his body could handle. It was very humid, and we had some heavy downpours and thunderstorms during the week, which made being in a camper with three dogs a bit unpleasant. We made it work, and all survived the week. Reflecting on the week, it turned out to be a really, good, and fun week. We made some good memories with the girls, and they still talk about it. It was the last vacation we had as a family.

Chapter 22

After our vacation, it was back to Fox Chase for another set of scans on August 29, 2016. He still looked good but continued with increasing fatigue and lack of appetite. Occasionally, he had issues with nausea and vomiting. He had lost another four pounds at this visit. All the tumors had enlarged, and there were some new tumors invading his lower back muscles into the *gluteus maximus*. He also had a moderate pleural effusion being reported, but no complaints of chest pain or shortness of breath. The pleural effusion reported several scans earlier had remained stable and of a small size this entire time.

His medication regimen was changed. He stopped the current medication, cabo, and started a new combination of Everolimus (which is what he had been taking after his first surgery, before the left kidney tumors appeared) combined with Lenvatinib. He was also placed on Marinol, a prescription form of marijuana to help stimulate his appetite and reduce nausea. He had some narcotic pain meds ordered but found they did not help much. The Marinol was not helping either. He resorted to smoking street marijuana in the garage, which helped a little with the nausea but only for a short time. It did not help much with his appetite or weight loss. It was certainly not the great cure that the pro-marijuana community claims it to be.

And I prayed that the weight loss would slow down. I prayed that the nausea would subside, and that this new combination of medications would slow his disease progression. We were not thrilled with him being back on the Everolimus as it did not help any in the early stage of his disease, but we were getting low on options. I prayed for peace and relief of both of our anxieties. My prayers started to change this past summer. Ecclesiastes 3 is "A Time for Everything" verses. Verse 6 is "a time to search and a time to give up." I did not give up on God, or on Paul, but I gave up on the idea of him being miraculously healed. My prayers became prayers of acceptance—acceptance that he was going to die of his disease, and that was God's plan. And prayers of relinquishment—that it was out of our control. We had fought in every way that was humanly available to us, but the evidence was in front of us that healing was not in His plan. He had limited time. He was losing his battle. I prayed that when death came that Paul did not suffer.

Chapter 22

I was still home, not yet cleared to return to work but was hopeful to be cleared at my next neurosurgical appointment mid-September. While at home this summer, we discussed a lot of life stuff. The hard stuff. The stuff no one wants to talk about and are not comfortable talking about. But it had to be done.

We had been discussing the need to make wills. Our former sister-in-law, Maureen, worked for an attorney office. I had said that I would call her sometime this week. Then I got that mental push, the same that I had when I cleaned and rearranged the basement and organized all our "important papers" files. I took the hint, that I attribute was a nudge from God, that I needed to get moving on this. I picked up the phone and called Maureen for a recommendation for an attorney that same evening.

We got our respective personal wills completed, along with power of attorney paperwork. Finalizing my will was the hardest, as mine had to include guardianship and care for our girls should I die before they were of legal age. Naming a guardian was something Paul and I had discussed from the time Kiersten was born. We were always torn about it though. People come and go in our lives, some for the better and some, not so much. It is a big responsibility on both parties. You know as a parent that no one is ever really going to replace you, and you do not want them to replace you. You also pray that it never comes to be needed. We casually asked Kiersten and Kaylee who they would choose to live with if that situation ever arises. They answered without hesitation, "Aunt Lori." We expected that answer, and she was our first choice anyway. Lori is the family member that I was closest with, and she is also the aunt that the girls were most connected to.

I also needed to appoint someone to oversee a trust fund. These were hard decisions as my family would expect to be included in some way. If I did not name someone in my family, they would resent it and possibly make it difficult for the person who was named. Making end of life wills, no matter your age, is not a pleasant thought process or a pleasant task, but it was a necessary task. I realized how fortunate we were that we had the time and opportunity to do this ahead of time. Some people are not given that time or may not take advantage of the time given them. And I prayed that we had made the right decisions. I also thanked God for the "push" to get it done and the time to do so.

The next item on the need-to-do-list was funeral concerns. What Paul wanted, where, and how. During our earlier boating years, we had a marina neighbor named Gary. When we bought our first home, we found out that Gary was now our neighborhood neighbor. Gary happened to be a funeral director at a funeral home a few blocks away. When I called him, he told me he was hoping to never have to get my phone call, but he was kind of expecting it. We met him at the funeral home a day or two later.

What a strange experience that was. To discuss your funeral while being alive is simply weird and unsettling. I know many people have planned out and pre-paid for burial plots, but it still was weird. Paul did not really care what was done or what cremation coffin was used as he was not going to know the difference at that point! I felt that I needed his input so I could fulfill his wishes when that time came. We took booklets home for the girls to pick out mini-urns and necklaces for his ashes. Not something they really understood at the time, but they picked colors and designs that appealed to them at that time.

Paul would talk to me about his wishes for our future. He wanted his ashes to stay at the house with us for at least a year before being placed in the ocean outside of Barnegat inlet. He made a list of stuff he wanted to give to his brothers, things he knew they would use or needed. We talked of selling the boats, the when and how and pricing.

Besides hoping and dreaming that he would be here for our future, he wanted us to be taken care of. He wanted me to finish my doctorate degree so that I could have more opportunities available to me in my career. He cried of how he did not want to leave us. Regardless of how independent I was, Paul did not want me and the girls to be alone. He wanted me to remarry at some time. He wanted the man to be a father figure to the girls, to fill in where he could not be. He gave permission to allow their last names to be changed if that was their desire. Gut-wrenching conversations that make me cry still. He then started naming men we knew who were single and who had children in the same age group that he thought would be a good match. I found it so strange that he would think this way while he was still alive, but it became a blessing for the future to be able to move on in a relationship without any guilt. It was what he wanted for me and for his girls.

Paul went back for more palliative radiation to shrink a tumor that had developed in the muscle of his back, between his shoulder blade and spine. It was causing him pain. It was the only time he really complained of anything hurting him, and he frequently would wince or suck in his breath. Peter accompanied him to his appointments. Paul could drive himself there and back, but it gave Peter a purpose—he was helping his brother and keeping him company.

And I prayed that we were making the correct decisions about everything. I thanked God for my recovery and Paul's continued presence. I prayed for peace from our fears and comfort for us all and easing of his pain.

Chapter 23

I would be cleared to return to work on September 20, 2016, at a part-time schedule. I arranged for our niece, Kelly to come to house in the morning and stay with her Uncle Paul until I came home around noon. He was still working but at a much-reduced schedule and mostly only fielding phone calls from home. He slept a lot and had a lot of anxiety. He was terribly thin, had no appetite, and was starting to tolerate less food. If he forced himself to eat, it would not stay down.

I was trying to keep as normal a schedule for the girls as I could. So much in our lives seemed out of our control, at least the routine could be controlled. I liked to think it helped ease the fears of the girls as they saw their dad getting worse, but I am not so sure of that now.

I would get them up, dressed, and dropped off at school like I used to do and head to work. Only now I was only working the morning hours. Paul readily agreed to having his niece with him in the morning for company. This continued four days a week for several months. It helped create a beautiful bond between the two of them that they would not otherwise have had.

I was glad to be well enough to return to work even if it was part time. It made me feel more normal. However, emotionally, physically, and mentally, I could only handle part time. I could not get through an entire day without a nap myself. My mental stamina was not back yet. Once I got tired, I could not focus and would have increased dizziness if I tried to push past the fatigue.

Some of that fatigue was because I was up frequently during the night with Paul. As his condition worsened, his anxiety and fear increased. We went to bed right after we put the kids to bed, but a few short hours later, he was up and pacing, then back to bed and up again the rest of the night.

The daylight hours were better for his anxiety. We would nap together when I came home from work, around noon, and get up so that I could pick the girls up from school. Kelly's presence was a blessing to us both.

Chapter 24

Paul continued to get worse with weight loss, fatigue, and vomiting. He tried to eat but nothing but a bite or two would stay down. He would take us out to dinner and would leave several times to vomit outside where no one would see or hear him.

We talked about options. Dr. P. had said she would always come into the office with a plan, but that forgoing treatment was also a plan. It was time to stop treatment. He was not feeling better with the medications, only feeling worse, and his cancer had marched right through everything we threw at it. We called Dr. P. and told her our decision to stop treatment and enter hospice. It was October 4, 2016. The way he looked, I was not sure he was going to make it to the end of the month. He did.

Four days later, on our twenty-second wedding anniversary, he drove himself to the marina to hang out and talk with whoever was around. He needed to get out of the house as the "walls were closing in on him."

The owners of the marina said they did a double take when they saw his truck pulling into the marina. They already knew he had started hospice. They were not sure how, or if it was even allowed, that someone on hospice was driving an hour to hang out at the marina. Paul felt if he was still breathing, he would go where he was the happiest, and the boat was his happy place.

It was time to sell the boats. We had barely made it through the summer boating season. I needed to sell the two boats while Paul was still here. He knew everything about them, inside and out, especially the big boat. I could certainly do it myself after his death, but I did not want to have to do it alone. We talked about it, and he agreed that at the end of the season (September to me but end of October to him), we would sell them. He wanted it settled so that I did not have to worry about it later, and it was another box to be checked off of things to be done.

We had an immediate buyer for the smaller boat, a friend of a marina friend. While we were sad to have to sell the little boat, we cried when we sold the big boat. We used a broker to list the big boat. We had interest in it right away, and after three weeks of negotiations, appraisals, and a water trial, it, too, was sold. We loved that boat. It was such a big part of our lives for so long and we had many great memories from it, as did the girls. It was hard seeing her pull away from the dock without either of us at the helm.

Paul took his brother Patrick and his friend Dave with him to the marina for the sea trial. Paul drove. Patrick and Dave were very relieved he was too tired to drive back and had handed the keys over. They later told me it was a fast and scary drive. I wanted one last ride on our boat, but due to a prior commitment with the girls, I could not make it to the marina for the sea trial.

The *Miss Guided III* sold easily, and the new owners took the boat to their new home in Florida. I later heard from the owner of our marina, that the *Miss Guided III* had been involved in a water rescue by the new owners in Florida. She saw it on a news report on the satellite TV in the marina office. She said the name was off the back of the boat, but there was no mistaking the radar arch and outriggers of the boat. She was a very seaworthy vessel, and I was glad to know she had made it into her new port. I am glad the new owners were now making their own great memories on that boat.

We were now into early November. Paul had made it to Halloween. I am not sure how he did it except through sheer determination. I prayed for his comfort and easing of his fears. I prayed for all our anxieties. I also prayed that he could hang in there for Thanksgiving.

Chapter 25

Paul looked sick and was not working except for fielding phone calls at home. His boss, G, was incredible. He kept Paul on the payroll, not only for the paycheck, but also so that we could keep the insurance benefits.

When G was a young boy and his own father became ill with cancer, he said it was done for his dad by his employer. It had a big impact on his family's' life, and he remembered the kindness. It was his way of paying it forward. Being the boss, he was able to do it, and he did it happily.

Paul made it to Thanksgiving. During this month we would get a hospital bed and a piano delivered in the same week! The hospital bed because it was part of the hospice package. The day it was delivered Paul, Kiersten, and Kaylee were lying on it together playing Xbox. I have a cute picture of it. We did not like what that bed represented, but we would come to need it.

Then the room began to smell, badly. I was blaming it on the dogs. I would clean the area rug in the living room and bathe the dogs, but still it smelled. Then I realized it was the mattress. Thankfully, I had layered the linens on the bed and had placed a mattress protector on it. I expected the mattress to have been cleaned and sanitized between patients. This one had escaped someone's notice.

I unzipped the mattress and found a foam mattress entirely soiled from diarrhea. I almost threw up thinking of this in my house and that we had all sat on that bed. Again, thankfully there were layers of bedding placed on it. It went out the door immediately. I then called the home care delivery company informing them of this situation. A new mattress was delivered the same day and apologies made but, yuck, that was just gross, and there is not any acceptable explanation for it to have happened.

The piano came because my church was looking to get rid of it due to a broken key, and I just happened to ask our pastor's wife about it before anyone else had. The caveat was that it needed to be out of the church foyer by Thanksgiving to allow room for preparations for our Christmas production. Both girls had been taking lessons from Mrs. W., a member of our church, for a few years and loved the idea of finally having a piano to practice on. I made delivery arrangements and it happened to coincide with the bed delivery, which I did not expect. It made for some interesting living room arrangement in our small ranch house.

With the hospice bed, oxygen supplies are also delivered. Paul used it sporadically at first, but by the end of November, he needed it most of the day. He absolutely needed it if he was walking around.

Chapter 26

He wore the oxygen to attend the girls school musical in early December. He looked so thin and frail by this time. The staff at the school and the parents noticed, too, and were surprised. They all knew our situation as the girls asked for prayer requests all the time, but they had not seen Paul for several months. His face was gaunt from the rapid weight loss which made his eyes appear large. His clothes were baggy, despite always having three layers on, due to cold intolerance. We did not stay for the entire musical. After Kiersten was finished playing percussion, we needed to leave as Paul did not have the stamina to stay.

Sometime during the early fall, we were chosen as the receiving family for a "Women with a Purpose" fundraiser. A member of my church was actively involved with this organization, and she, along with some of her friends, nominated us, and we were picked to be their next "cause." The dinner fundraiser was held on December 4, 2016, at a local venue called The Stone Terrace. They were prepared for one hundred people. Over two hundred people showed up. It was amazing and humbling. The staff at the restaurant acted as if they were prepared for this many people all along, and they just kept bringing more food out to serve. They remained so cool and efficient, and it was impressive.

Paul attended, with his oxygen, but could not stay for the entire event. He was so tired and was barely able to stay standing beyond a few minutes. He was overwhelmed with the amount of people there. Paul was starting to show signs of confusion. He did not understand the purpose of the organization or how it came about that we were the guests of honor. He was confused at the amount of people in attendance as he recognized few of them.

There were people from church, our neighborhood, our school, our families, and of course, the women who attend the events as part of the organization. I had not heard of this organization before this, but apparently, many others knew of the organization. I was shocked that word had reached so many. I was humbled at the turnout and generosity of so many and thought of it as another blessing.

December 4 was also Kiersten's eleventh birthday. We had a simple celebration at home with her. I made her a chocolate cake per her request. She opened her gifts, and all was good for the moment.

Paul determined that if he made it to Thanksgiving, he would make it to Kiersten's birthday. If he made it to Kiersten's birthday, he would make it to Christmas and then Kaylee's birthday on January 5. After that, there were no more milestones to make. As I already stated, he was getting confused at times, but it made for some interesting conversations and some difficult evenings. During the day, he was oriented and coherent. The evenings would bring anxiety, agitation and confusion. This, along with some nighttime wandering would only get worse over the coming weeks.

Chapter 27

I did not want Paul to drive anymore. He had always been an aggressive driver, but now, he did not seem to be in control of the vehicle. He could not determine the speed he was at and his visual perception was not right. He drove a three-quarter-ton Dodge, diesel, extended cab, long-bed pickup. This was a big truck. If he hit someone with this truck, it was going to cause damage and injury.

Shortly before Christmas, we were going to his parent's house for dinner. He wanted to take the truck as he needed fuel but needed to get cash from the bank first. I suggested that I drive, but he just looked at me like I was crazy. While I had driven his truck many times, if he was capable, he was driving.

I voiced my concerns, which he felt were not valid, so he drove to the bank and to the gas station, erratically. All we could do was scream. He just missed the tree in the bank parking lot as he was going too fast and could not turn the truck enough. He then scraped the truck on the yellow concrete post in front of the ATM.

We left the bank parking lot, and he took a right turn onto the next street, again too fast, and crossed into oncoming traffic. Instead of correcting his turn and slowing down, he made a fast left into the gas station, cutting off the oncoming minivan and hitting the rear corner of a parked pickup truck in the gas station. He then pulled the truck up to the pump, placed it in park, and gave me the keys.

The owner of the damaged truck came over and was, of course, disgruntled. Paul started talking nonsense, offering to buy the guy's truck outright (not sure how or with what money) or have it completely scrapped! This guy thought Paul was on drugs. He was the mechanic at the station and was clearly insulted by Paul's suggestion to "scrap" his truck, and he was getting angrier by the second.

I got his attention and told him what was happening and was able to deflate the situation. The guy took a good look at Paul and asked how old he was. I told him he was forty-six. I could see the shock in his face and his anger just evaporated. I gave him my contact information so that I could reimburse him for the busted taillight. He shook my hand and wished me luck. Being a mechanic, I am sure he changed the light himself as I never heard from him about the cost of the taillight.

Chapter 28

Paul was always checking the temperature setting on the thermostat. It was programmable, but he just could not help himself and had to stop and play with it every time he passed it. He grew up with a father who was also always adjusting the thermostat to save pennies. Paul was still trying to fiddle with the thermostat settings but could no longer clearly see the numbers on the thermostat. I would find it at 86 one day and then 54 on another day. So now I had to remind myself to keep checking the temperature setting as he was randomly hitting the up or down buttons.

He was also obsessed with wires. He would try to unplug every cord he saw. The hospice bed became a constant thing needing to be fixed. Despite his condition, he was able to flip the bed frame on its side and attempt to re-wire it. He was unplugging the power cord from the wall and the bed and then plugging it back in after hitting the buttons on the control. He got satisfaction when I would show him it was now working, that he had fixed it. It would, however, upset the girls as they thought he was going to hurt himself. This became a daily ritual, but it was still scary to see him flip the bed. Trying to stop him only made him more agitated.

He started wandering at night. I would wake up, see that he was not in bed and walk the house to find him. I found him one night outside on our concrete front steps. He had fallen onto his right side, the same side he had the rib metastasis. He was not able to get up on his own. It was nine degrees outside, and he was only in his underwear. He was trying to get something from the garage but was not able to tell me what he needed from the garage at two in the morning. I do not know how long he was there, but his skin was very cold.

Peter came over the next day and put a door alarm on the front and back doors so it would wake me up. He fell often during his wanderings. As he came back down the hallway to come to bed, I would wake up as I could hear him picking up speed. It was like a locomotive, at first shuffling and then getting faster as he stumbled into the bedroom. He would fall onto the floor, into the closet or into the nightstand just as I scrambled out of bed to try to catch him. I was always a few seconds too late. He had scrapes and bruises everywhere.

The girls had painted pictures for him when he was in the hospital during the brain surgery. Two of the paintings were houses, one big, one small. One day, he called Kiersten into the bedroom. He had placed these pictures on the bed and was calling them the blueprints for our new house. He proceeded to tell Kiersten that the big one was going to be our house in Australia and the little one was the doghouse he was going to build for Lincoln and Opie. She just stood there smiling, looking confused and amused, as she did not know what else to do. She still laughs when she recalls this story.

When she talked about it later that night, I talked to the girls on how to react to their dad when he was saying abnormal things. I told them to just go along with him, shake their heads, smile, and "yes, Dad" him. If they tried to correct him, he just got angry and cursed at them.

I would have the girls keep an eye on him while I was making dinner. If he started doing something that could hurt him, they had to yell for me. Kaylee took this job seriously. She would hide, sneak behind furniture, and peek in doorways to spy on him. Sometimes he would catch her, and his reaction varied each time. The one that stands out the most to Kaylee was during one of the times she found him pulling on wires and came to tell me. He knew he was going to be in trouble and tried to stop her. He raised a fist at her and called her a little "b" word. It completely shocked her and frightened her. She was hurt that he called her that but can also laugh at it now. Kaylee reminded me of another story while I was writing this. This story makes her laugh. It made me laugh too, yet I feel bad that I did not know it happened.

Apparently, one night in his wanderings through the house, Paul decided he wanted her bed. Kaylee said she was asleep and it was dark. Her dad came into the room and pulled her by the ankle out of bed and onto the floor saying that he was sleeping in her bed. She said it, did not scare her, and she slept on the carpet of her room. She did not care that she was on the floor as she sometimes slept in her sleeping bag on the floor to "camp." She recalls it with humor, and for her, it is a happy memory.

He was often very cold and would dress in layers. As the weeks progressed, he would put on whatever he found. He liked his underwear drawer and would layer underwear under his clothes, on top of his clothes and on his head. Other times I would come home from the work, and he would be wearing my fleece pajamas. It was sad that they fit him better than me with his weight loss. He would open dresser drawers and put on whatever he saw that felt soft. He came up with some interesting and funny outfits some days.

He was now under 150 pounds. At his heaviest, he weighed over 300 pounds. When he was diagnosed with cancer, he weighed around 205 pounds. This was also after having had weight loss surgery. He would continue to lose weight steadily.

Chapter 29

The week of Christmas, 2016 (after the school musical), he was determined to buy the girls an Xbox One. He knew I could have cared less about another gaming system despite both girls asking for it. They already had an Xbox 360, and that was enough from my perspective. When he said it was his last Christmas and he really wanted to get it for them, I had to agree. He insisted on going to the store with me even though he felt awful that morning. He wanted to be the one to get it, not just say it was a gift from him.

The GameStop store is only a few miles from our house and usually takes less than ten minutes to get there. It took us closer to twenty-five minutes to get there this morning. Not because of traffic, as it was before 9:00 a.m., but because I had to keep pulling over to the side of the road for him to vomit. His nausea and vomiting were escalating despite meds to treat it. But the motion sickness was new.

We made it to the store just after opening and already there was a line. We were fourth in line, but it was slow moving. There was a woman talking on her cell phone two people ahead of us. It was annoying to hear her loud conversation, but Paul was really annoyed by it. He was barely standing and continued to be nauseous, so his patience level was nonexistent. He started making comments about smacking her in the head to shut her up, and he was not subtle about it. I do not think she heard him over the sound of her own loud voice, but the lady directly in front of us did. She turned to us and said that she was glad she was not the one on the phone he was directing his comment to. I was telling him to behave himself and to keep quiet just as she turned and looked at Paul. She took in his appearance and gave me a sympathetic smile. Anyone could see he was not well, and it seemed to give him a "get out of jail free" pass. He got the Xbox One system and we painstakingly made our way back home, with several stops on the side of the road.

He made it to Christmas. It was bittersweet. We were happy he was still with us, and we embraced every moment, but it was sad knowing it was his last Christmas with us all. His mom was doing better but was suffering from memory loss due to brain radiation. She had brain radiation to prevent the lung cancer from attacking her brain, a common occurrence. But when radiation is generalized, as her radiation treatments were, it causes hair and memory loss. When the radiation is applied to a very distinct area of the brain, you may get some hair loss in that spot but not the memory issues.

We did our usual Christmas celebrations. We spend Christmas Eve with his family, and then Christmas evening the girls and I have dinner with my family. This was the first time in several years that Paul came with me to my parents' house. Overall, it was probably one of our best Christmases together as he was the most present and engaged with the family. He had a sad and lost look, which was easily seen in the photographs of that day. He was so tired but pushed through it for the few hours at his parents' house.

And I prayed that he could hang in there just ten more days until Kaylee's birthday. He was determined and his will to live compensated a lot for his physical condition. His cognitive decline was bad, and his bouts of confusion were more consistent and throughout the day, but he did have times of complete clarity too. He no longer remembered our names, but he knew who we were. He was still walking but needed a steadying hand. He was barely eating anything beyond one to two bites and not able to drink much either.

Chapter 30

Kaylee's birthday is January 5. Paul had made it this far. He was a bit scratched up and bruised as he had fallen the night before, hitting his face on the nightstand. But he was there. We had a quiet dinner and cake at home. It was a celebration of her birth but also his ability to still be present with us. Without any more milestones to attain, I worried how much longer he could fight.

I was still enrolled in my doctorate program. I was taking one class at a time and praying my way through the program. I often questioned if I should even be doing this. It seemed selfish to work on research for school when time was limited for Paul. However, he really wanted this for me. It was his way of helping me secure additional career opportunities for the future.

I had another paper assigned. I do not remember which class it was or the exact details of the assignment, but I used my current situation to guide my topic. I wanted to find out more about delirium in cancer patients at end of life. I needed some guidance on what else to expect and wanted some explanations as to the process that was occurring, beyond what I was reasoning it to be. I was able to write my paper and look for answers to help me with Paul.

My research efforts identified a gap in knowledge for nursing research. Everything I was finding on the topic applied to an older population or general delirium and its reversible causes. There was nothing specific to cancer patients in Paul's age group with delirium. There was nothing that I found to help me answer the questions I was asking. I tucked that away for a while but would bring it up later to the hospice nurse, who also had no insight for me.

Pastor Emmons had been coming to the house to visit with Paul since December, when Paul just could not tolerate sitting in church anymore. He needed to get up frequently at least twice during the sermon to vomit, and I was afraid he would fall. Paul continually asked him to read 2 Corinthians 5:1–10. It was a section he had latched onto that brought him peace and comfort. He would ask me to read it to him often through the week, he just could not remember the verse, only the "one about the new heavenly body."

One day in February, Paul asked pastor to baptize him. During this visit, Paul was in his hospice bed and could not get up. He was asleep more than he was awake this week. Pastor Emmons just kept on reading scripture and talking to Paul. Paul would grunt and open his eyes and then close them again. At one point, he opened his eyes widely and asked to be baptized.

Paul was baptized as an infant in his mom's church. Baptism is a public pronouncement of your belief in Jesus Christ. We, in the Baptist faith, decide to be baptized when one is old enough to make that assertion on your own behalf. Paul, despite being new to his faith, was able to grasp this understanding and ask for it. Pastor looked at me with an expression that read "How are we going to do this?"

At his request, I got him a glass of water, and he baptized Paul while on his hospice bed. I had also been baptized as an infant, as had my girls (as our families had expected it), but I had not taken the steps to do an adult baptism despite knowing the reasons for it in the Bible. I decided that day, that if my husband, in his weakened state and with his brain not fully functioning could see the importance of this declaration of his faith, then I needed to do so too.

I told the girls what had happened that day when they came home from school. They were excited to know this took place and wished they had been there for it. We agreed as a family that we would participate in the next baptism event offered at the church which would take place Easter Sunday.

When he had spurts of energy, he would ask to help him walk outside in front of the house, regardless of the cold. Sometime the next week just before the hospice nurse arrived, Paul said he had to get out of the house. He would not let me help him and he walked next door to Merinda's house. Merinda is our neighbor and the kids' adopted grandmother. We love Merinda. She has been a blessing to us and our girls and is still a big part of our lives. He walked into her house saying, "That woman is driving me nuts."

Merinda asked him, "Who is driving you nuts?" and all he could do was point toward our house saying, "That woman," since he could not remember my name, again. It took her a few moments to catch on to what he was saying and who he was referring to. She still chuckles over that short visit.

He could not stay long as his hospice nurse John had arrived. John examined Paul and pronounced that his blood pressure and pulse were still stable and strong despite his physical deterioration and lack of oral intake. Paul was skeletal at this time as his ability to tolerate anything was even worse than before and he would just vomit it back up. John looked at me and shook his head not understanding how or what was keeping him going.

The next day was a Friday. My work schedule has been Monday through Thursday for the past ten years. I got the kids to school and came back, and Paul was still sleeping. He had fallen asleep in the early morning hours in the hospice bed, which was unusual. He did not like staying in the hospice bed for too long as it scared him. He was usually back and forth between the bedroom and living room all night long, which is only a short hallway as we lived in a small ranch house.

Around 11:00 a.m., he started stirring, and I saw he was covered in sweat. His eyes were open but not focused, and he was not able to talk or walk on his own. I got him out of bed and put him on my back to carry him to the bathroom. I put him in the shower chair and washed the sweat off him. He slowly got his bearings, but still could not talk to me, only shaking his head. I was able to leave him under the shower while I quickly changed the bed, got him dressed and back into bed. He got better over the next hour and perked up and was able to support himself when getting up but was unsteady.

He kept wanting to go to the bathroom to urinate but would stand there a few seconds as if going through the motions, say he was done or that he could not go. After a few times of this, I realized I am taking him to the bathroom, but he had not urinated, at all. It made me think, hard, of when was the last time I heard him urinate and realized it had been at least twenty-four hours. I knew his battle was coming to a quick end. When the kidneys shut down, it is a matter of a few days before the fluids and toxins build up in your body and death ensues. The waiting and watching of what I knew was coming was now staring at me. Death was hovering, and I felt like I could see it, just waiting for that last weak moment to take over.

Saturday, he awoke and again, could not speak and could not support himself. He was very agitated and would not stay still. We traveled from the bed to the sofa back to the bed every two minutes, but I had to totally support him when standing. At one time, he started swaying with me, and I jokingly asked him if he was trying to dance with me. He started to hum and held me a bit tighter and then did start to dance with me. It was sweet and sad, yet I cherish the moment.

By lunchtime, I had to call in reinforcements. I was exhausted and needed help. He still was not talking, could not walk on his own, and would not stay seated for more than one minute. I could not leave him alone because he would try to get up and fall. The kids tried to help, but they were not strong enough to hold him up. They helped distract him so I could at least use the bathroom.

Peter, Lori, and Patrick arrived shortly after calling them. They, too, were exhausted within the hour and could not believe I had already been doing this for a few hours before they arrived. Despite his general weakness, he fought his brothers as they tried to restrain him from getting back up from the sofa again. They were just trying to catch their breath.

Patrick wanted a picture taken of the three of them on the sofa. When I look at that picture, it makes me want to cry every time because it truly is an awful photo, yet I cannot let it go. I joke that it looks like a scene from the movie *Weekend at Bernie's*. It reminds me of how sick he was at the end and that he is now in the presence of Jesus.

I called the hospice emergency line and the nurse on call for the weekend arrived an hour later to assess the situation. She then called for an aid to come to the house for the next twenty-four hours as she saw our exhaustion. The nursing assistant arrived around dinner and was instructed to give him alternating doses of Ativan and Haldol to control the agitation, anxiety, and restlessness.

Kiersten did not want to stay at home and left to have a sleep over at Uncle Peter's house with her cousin, PJ. Kaylee wanted to be home. I sent the rest of the family home for the night.

After getting Kaylee to bed, the nursing assistant gave me strict instructions to get some rest. She was on duty and would care for Paul, and I was to stay in bed until the morning and ignore any sounds coming from the living room. It was a fitful sleep because I expected her to knock on the bedroom door with bad news, but that did not happen. I awoke before 6:00 a.m. and quickly showered but was afraid of what I would find when I went in the living room.

As I entered the living room, I saw that Paul was in the bed with labored breathing, and I could hear the fluid in his lungs with every breath. The aid told me she fought with him all night. He was agitated, confused, restless, and tried most of the night to get out of bed. The Ativan doses had finally caught up to him to sedate him and keep him still. It took the fight out of him and was allowing the natural process of his illness to take over.

I started to wash his face and lips. His mouth was dry, and there was still some residue from the medication in his mouth. I automatically did the usual care of a nurse for her patient, but this time, it was a wife for her dying husband. The final acts of caring for him. And I talked to him, telling him I loved him, and it was okay to stop fighting. The girls and I had everything we needed.

Soon, Pete and Lori arrived. Kaylee awoke and came out to the living room and said she wanted to leave and go to Uncle Peter's house to be with her sister and cousins. Pete got her packed up and out the door. Kaylee remembers this day well. She regrets that she did not actually say goodbye to her dad before leaving the house, except a "Bye, Dad" as she went out the door. She was afraid as she knew something bad was happening. I have told her that he would not want you to remember him as he was that morning. I am sure he heard you say goodbye to him. It did not give her much solace.

Lori heard his breathing and I remember her saying, "Oh, brother." She turned music on and started singing to him to cover up the "death rattle" sounds, knowing that listening to that noise would drive us insane. When Patrick arrived a short time later, I had him walk the dogs with me as I needed a short break. He was glad for the distraction too.

Pete called his parents to tell them to get dressed so he could pick them up. He returned to the house around 11:00 a.m. I saw the car pull to the curb and announced that Mom and Dad were here. I was sitting alongside the bed holding Paul's hand and saw his breathing change. Mom was just coming into the house, but Dad had stopped for a smoke. I yelled to Peter to get dad in here. Now.

They took my place by his side, and I moved to his feet, rubbing them. His breathing turned to what we call agonal. It is a reflex action at the time of death. On his last breath, as I told him to "Go in peace, go to God," he said, "God" and stopped breathing. Paul died on Sunday, February 19, 2017, at the age of forty-six at 11:10 a.m.

Chapter 31

I called our neighbor, Gary, the funeral director. He came right over to wait with us for the transport car to arrive. Lori and I helped transfer Paul to the gurney, our last act of caring for him, wrapping him up in the bedsheets from home and kissing him goodbye. We cried but thanked God he was at peace, and he had not been in any pain.

I wanted to put the house back in order and get all the medical equipment out of there before bringing the kids home. It took only a few minutes to accomplish this with the help of Lori, Patrick, and Janet. We all needed something to do. It was over, and we felt lost. Patrick put the hospice bed and other medical stuff in the driveway and called the company for pickup. Janet vacuumed—apparently a favorite of hers—and Lori and I moved the furniture back into place.

Once Peter returned from taking his parents home, it was time to go to his house and tell all the kids. It went better than expected as they knew what was happening, it was just a matter of what time it would happen. Both of my girls expressed that they were glad they had been with their cousins and not at home during this time. The reality of their dad being gone would hit once they came home. It was a solemn night and lots of tears. But the sun was shining in the morning, and they wanted to go back to their cousins for the day.

Lori and I went to meet with the funeral director to finalize arrangements. The obituary was already completed and only needed a date of death and funeral arrangements added to it. Paul and I had written the obituary shortly after meeting with Gary during the summer to arrange the funeral.

The services would take place over two days as we expected a large turnout due to his union involvement. I wanted it done as soon as possible, not have it drag out. Since we were able to make the submission deadline for the newspaper, the funeral services would be held Tuesday evening and Wednesday morning. With that arranged early in the morning, we needed a distraction.

We went shopping. I had wanted to replace the living room furniture for over a year, but life had more pressing issues for me to handle. I also hated our bed. It was an old free-flow waterbed—yes, a waterbed. Paul loved it because it was warm. I had long ago out-grown it!

The mattress had been upgraded over the years, and I had bought a new headboard/footboard that we modified to accommo-date the sides of the waterbed, but it was still a waterbed. I needed to also find wood bed frame supports that connected the headboard and footboard as Paul threw out the ones that came with the bed-room set. They were up in the loft in the garage with my holiday décor boxes, and he was mad about something and threw them away because they were "taking up too much space." Meanwhile, in the garage, you couldn't walk because he had enough things in there to restock a Home Depot store.

I took Lori to Boscov's. It was one of my favorite stores, and she had never been there. She could not imagine that it had a furni-ture department. We had so much fun. Especially when it came to finding a mattress. The poor salesman probably thought we were a lesbian couple. We tried out every mattress, telling each other to "roll the other way" or "this one does not suck."

I ended up buying a mattress and box spring, new sofa and two club chairs. One of which Lori claimed as hers for when she comes over. Boscov's did not have the bedframe rails that I needed. I would need to go to another furniture store to find what I needed, but first, lunch.

We went back to my house for lunch. While there, I started typing up the eulogy. I had a patient tell me that she did her spouse's eulogy because, as he put it, "Who else would have known me bet-ter?" It gave me pause. I asked Paul about it that day once I got home.

He told he fully expected me to give the eulogy. Anyone else could say what they wanted too.

My first attempt was terrible. It showed a lot of misplaced anger toward my family and was just not appropriate for the time, place, or event. Once I started over, with a clearer headspace, the words just flowed, and it came to be written in less than an hour. Lori was my test audience, editor, and approver.

Chapter 32

Then we remembered we needed to find flowers for the casket and funeral home. Despite being tired, I needed to keep moving. I was restless sitting there at home, and Lori was stuck to me like glue. If I fed Lori coffee, she was good to go. We ordered flowers from the local Shoprite on the recommendation of the funeral home. They did a fantastic job, and the price was very reasonable.

I was not ready to go back home. It was too quiet despite Lori's company. The kids were with Uncle Peter and would come home after we all had dinner together.

I figured while we were up and out, let's go to a furniture store to look for the bed rails. We got lucky and the manager knew exactly what I was looking for. He was able to locate the style I wanted in a stain/color that was close enough. Bonus, it was in stock at the store.

The salesman always hangs around with the customer until they are done at the checkout desk. I had told him I needed the side rails as my husband had thrown the original set away since we were not using them. To make small talk, he made a statement about making sure your husband does not throw these rails away.

The poor man had no idea about what had just occurred, and I felt that he did not need to know about it, either. Lori and I just looked wide-eyed at each other. We reassured the salesman that we were positive that he would not be throwing this set away. It made us chuckle on the way home.

I did not want the kids at the funeral home the first night. I knew that it was going to be a long evening. I had my parents come to house to stay with them. And I prayed for the strength, physically and mentally to get through the next two days. I prayed for my children.

The turnout was incredible and the line of people arriving to pay their respects to us, and Paul, stretched out the door and down the street for three hours. Old friends, coworkers, and acquaintances showed up in support of each of us. The receiving line consisted of me, Lori and Peter, Patrick, and Janet. Mom and Pop Schroeder were there and handling things better than expected. Mom clearly enjoyed the interaction with some of her former coworkers and close friends, and she stayed in the middle of the room catching up with them.

We each had people from our individual lives turn out to give us support. My old Allstate Insurance agents even showed up, and they had left the company a few years prior to start their own insurance agency! Pastors from my church and from the kids' school showed up, as well as most of the teachers and even some of the parents and students. The amount of love and support and kind words that were shared that night, and the next morning, was overwhelming, uplifting, and humbling at the same time.

Dad, however, wanted to leave partway through and asked Peter to take him home. His advancing Alzheimer's left him restless, anxious, and his coping mechanism was to lay down and sleep. I had medicated Dad with an Ativan, left over from Paul's supply from hospice. It helped, but not completely.

Peter told him he was not leaving his brother's funeral to take him home and gave him an option. Peter would find someone to take him home or he could pull up a chair and close his eyes. He was angry with Peter that he would not leave the funeral to take him home. When he realized that Peter was serious and not taking him home, he agreed to have someone else take him home. Peter arranged for Lori's parents to drive him home and stay with him until he was settled. It was a long, tiring evening, and we had to do it again the next morning.

During the viewing, Lori pointed out to me that Paul was blowing bubbles! She had been going over to the casket, casually, to wipe his mouth as bubbles kept forming. She had done it often enough that her daughter wanted to know why she kept wiping Uncle Paul's mouth.

We told the funeral director. He and the other director were mortified this was happening and did not know why. As nurses, we just assumed it was a release of some gas/chemical process going on. Or as a friend, also a nurse, put it, he was either blowing kisses our way or trying to spit on those people he did not like! We were highly amused, as nurses have a strange sense of humor anyway, but the funeral director was not. We kept our laughter to ourselves after that! By the next morning, whatever process had been occurring had stopped and Paul was no longer blowing bubbles.

Chapter 33

The morning started out as the night before had ended, a large turn-out. The room was full. The kids were doing well. Kaylee did not want to approach the casket saying, "That is not my dad anymore. His spirit is in heaven, that is just his body." Kiersten approached the casket several times, though briefly. I let them determine what they could handle, as my pediatrician suggested. They mostly stayed in the rear side of the room, hanging out with their cousins, and looking at the photo albums.

I gave the eulogy. That was followed by a service from our pastor. I think the eulogy nicely summarized our relationship, Paul's personality and his interests and new faith. I recited the verse he clung to from 2 Corinthians 5:1–5. I concluded the eulogy with, "Enjoy your new heavenly body, Paul. You will be missed," as the tears welled up and my voice cracked.

I held the repast at Mercer Oaks, a golf club. The owner of the catering services at the club, Jim had asked me to call him when the time came. He offered the use of the ballroom and his staff to cater and host the post-funeral meal. The food was fantastic, and all went so smoothly.

A family friend, who lived across the street from Paul's family growing up, Mrs. Z., approached Jim and insisted on covering a portion of the catering costs. Jim tried to politely decline her offer, but he was outmaneuvered! Mrs. Z. not only paid for a portion of the event, but she also donated a generous check to my girls.

The following week, the girls returned to school. I stayed home a bit longer before returning to work, full-time now. The house was quieter and simply weird. All the busyness of Paul's care was now done, the new furniture had arrived, and the house was in order.

We seemed to be managing, but it was just actions. I still had my days sectioned into groups of hours, the morning and then the afternoon/evening. I could not plan for anything beyond a day at a time, putting one foot in front of the other, feeling numb. It got better over the next several weeks. Danny Gokey's song, "Tell Your Heart to Beat Again" was released around this time and popular on Christian radio. It became our anthem song, and we would turn it up and sing it loud with tears in our eyes every time it played.

I had promised Paul that I would continue with my doctorate schooling, so I continued to plod my way through. It was hard to concentrate that quarter of school and into the next quarter, but I persisted, and slowly it became easier. Just being busy was easier. I continued to pray my way through the program. The teachers at the girl's school were vigilant in praying for my family and keeping watch on the girls for any adjustment issues.

In April, after the spring break fares dropped, I scheduled a four-day weekend at Universal Studios. This was my first step in making any plans beyond twenty-four hours. I prayed my way through the planning and into the trip that if it were His will, He would allow this to occur; if not, send me a signal, loudly and clearly. Nothing happened to stop our trip, and it turned out to be great.

While we had gone to Disney twice, we had never made it to Universal. It was a trip that I had discussed with Paul when he entered hospice. He encouraged me to make the trip after his death to unwind and recenter. It was strange and bittersweet to be there without him. We talked of him a lot during our visit to the parks and thoroughly enjoyed our time there. The trip was easy, crowd levels were low, and we had beautiful weather. It was great and sad at the same time.

I also booked a Disney cruise for early summer for our vacation. Again, something I had discussed with Paul, before the cancer took over his brain function. He wholeheartedly agreed that I should do this while I had the money available and to enjoy life and make memories with the girls. Again, I felt like it was a leap of faith to plan out this cruise. I again, prayed my way through the planning of the trip. I was no longer getting through my days in chunks of hours and was able to plan day by day.

We sailed on the Disney Fantasy for their western Caribbean cruise. We arrived the day before the sail date to stay overnight at Disney's Art of Animation resort to enjoy the pools and relax. I did not want to worry about airport delays and miss the cruise. I did not worry about the cost of anything on this trip. I was all about just being present and trying to relax and let Disney take care of everything.

We had such a great time. We swam with the dolphins in Grand Cayman (my bucket list item), did stingray beach and snorkeled with reef sharks and stingrays in Cozumel, and did the lazy river in Jamaica. We fell in love with the people of Jamaica and vowed to return, whether by cruise or plane, to further explore this beautiful island and its flavorful people.

It took me the third day on the cruise ship to realize that I could relax. I found my peace with a lounge chair on the adult deck overlooking the seas while the kids played in the pool. They checked in with me at designated times. They loved the freedom to not have me watching them every minute. I realized that I needed the time too. I had no idea the amount of tension I was holding in and the unending horizon of water rolling by during the day at sea allowed me to speak to God and admit the pain of my loss and let go of the grief and guilt.

Yes, guilt. Even though I did all that I could as a wife and nurse for Paul, there is still guilt that maybe I could have done something more or something better, prayed more or prayed more urgently/emphatically/faithfully. There are always doubts. This, in addition to the doubts of parenting, and trying my best to guide my kids through a situation for which there is no rulebook to guide you. Guilt that I was trying to enjoy life, even though I had Paul's full blessing and encouragement to live life to its fullest, to play, to travel and love again.

We returned home having loved every moment of our trip. It was still June, and we had another two months of summer. I booked us a two-night, three-day stay in a hotel in Ocean City, New Jersey for later in the summer. It was perfect except Kaylee broke her arm and was in a cast. With the use of a watertight rubber cast cover, we enjoyed the beach and pool time. The girls both got hermit crabs, something I had been putting off buying for years. They kept asking for hermit crabs every summer when we would visit any boardwalk, and this year I caved in and they got them. They named them Pinkeye and Marshmallow.

We clung tight to our family traditions with Paul's family, and we try to continue the traditions several years later. Thanksgiving remained structured the same, with some allowances for meal prep due to the declining health and mental faculties of both Dad and Mom Schroeder. The same at Christmas. We managed to get through the year of "firsts" better than I expected. And I prayed for us to continue to not only, survive, but thrive. I prayed continually for my girls, that they remain healthy and strong. And I prayed especially for Mom and Pop Schroeder. Their health was declining quickly.

Chapter 34

During the summer following Paul's death, Kiersten's hamster died. We got another hamster shortly after. Then Kaylee's hamster died in my hand. We think she fell from the second level of her cage and suffered head trauma. This poor creature lay in my hand gasping for breath for a few minutes until she stopped breathing. Then, the newest hamster died after our summer vacation.

During the summer, Opie, our special needs English Mastiff, started falling more often. His left leg seemed to be getting weaker. I knew at some point the lesion in his neck would move and cause more weakness or even paralysis of his hind legs. I was fortunate that Opie had made it into adulthood. He was now eight years old.

One day in October, he went off the back porch steps and fell. He could not keep his legs under him after that. He had reinjured his weaker leg, and now he was struggling to stay standing. I used a sling under his hips to help him back into the house. I medicated him with doggie anti-inflammatories and waited until morning to see how he was.

He was not any better. I called around for some lifting help. Opie weighed 180 pounds. Peter and a neighbor came over late morning to help load Opie into the car for his final trip to the vet. The girls were able to say goodbye to him that morning. They knew it was time for him to go. They saw him fall and saw that he was in pain. The vet confirmed that he had reinjured his leg, but he also had swelling and a possible tumor on his toes of that same leg. She, too, felt the neck lesion had progressed, and there was nothing more to be done for Opie. Peter had accompanied me to the emergency vet and stayed with me as we euthanized Opie. Oh, how my heart broke, again.

Before this happened, I had visited a local acupuncturist to get relief of my stress headaches. There I met a woman, an intake person, who interviewed me, asked me reasons for seeking acupuncture and explained the type of acupuncture done at that practice. While she was interviewing me, she said, "I am sorry, but your husband keeps interrupting me." She is a psychic and asked if I wanted her to continue. She started relaying things "Paul was saying." She told me many things that made me cry through my acupuncture session but also gave me comfort. Without knowing anything about Opie, as I had not mentioned my dogs, she said, "Paul says not to worry about the dog, he will be fine."

I did not know anything about this woman's abilities before making this appointment. I would not have sought out a "psychic" on my own. I felt that God led me there for a specific message to be delivered. I returned for a few more acupuncture sessions but never had another encounter with this woman.

And I thanked God for leading me there, for whatever purpose. The acupuncture treatments did not help much, but my encounter with the "psychic" intake person had given me some comfort. I prayed for my kids, their grief at so much loss in one year. I prayed for healing of our hearts.

Chapter 36

I had a mammogram done in December. It showed increased calcifications in the right breast. I needed to go back for additional mammogram films. No big deal. I have had this same discussion with many women over the years while working in internal medicine and ordering mammograms, additional mammogram images and/or ultrasounds for some.

The radiologist said I have had calcifications present on prior mammograms, but these were new and in the "gray zone." Meaning, not cancer but not sure they are completely benign either. I needed a mammotome, or biopsy, done. I went to a surgeon who I have known, and referred others to, for years.

A mammotome was performed January 2018, and Dr. D. felt that this would likely be benign as 70 percent of calcifications are not cancerous. It showed a pre-cancer or DCIS (ductal carcinoma in-situ). I was then scheduled for a lumpectomy of the affected area at the end of January. I got a call from my surgeon the following week, the first week of February. He said he "could not believe he had to tell me this, but the DCIS was indeed present, but in the middle of that tissue was also a small area of cancerous cells." I officially had breast cancer.

I was at work when I got this phone call. I cried; my fellow office staff members cried with me. I went home and stomped around and cursed and yelled. And then I prayed for guidance. I prayed for God's peace and mercy. I felt that "peace of God that surpasses all understanding" written in Philippians 4:7. While on my knees that afternoon, I knew that I had to walk through the fire of treatment, but I had a calmness, a peace, telling me that I would come out the other side fine. It truly is beyond understanding and hard to explain as it is a feeling deep in your gut that is otherworldly. I did not have any anxiety going into the chemotherapy treatments or radiation or starting the Tamoxifen. I do not have any anxiety about my cancer. I do not worry that every new ache/pain/ or new symptom is because of my cancer or a return of the cancer. I occasionally worry that it could return when I learn of others who have had a reoccurrence, but it is a fleeting thought.

I would now need another lumpectomy and removal of the sentinel lymph node. This is done to see if the cancer has made its way into the lymph nodes under the armpit. Considering that this was caught so early, it was unlikely, but needed to be confirmed. They were negative for cancer.

I have vowed to remove February off the calendar for all future years (if that were possible). February 2014 is when Paul's cancer was found in his other kidney. February 2015 Paul's cancer spread to his lungs. February 2016, I had the brain tumor. February 2017 was when Paul died, and now February 2018, I have cancer. This year would start out poorly but would end well. The second half of 2018 was like the decline on a roller coaster after the first big drop. Things happened quickly, but for the better.

And then, how do I tell my girls? Oh man, oh man, oh man, that was a tough one, and I was on my knees praying for guidance and wisdom. Kiersten did not say too much. Kaylee, however (now nine years old), stated very matter-of-factly that "my dad died of cancer and now mom has it and I am going to be an orphan and go live with Aunt Lori." Wow. I had to do some fast talking to explain the differences in our cancers and to reassure Kaylee that I was not going to die. And I prayed some more about how to reassure them and calm their fears, as well as my own.

Since my cancer was a stage 1, I decided to stay local for treatment. I met with Dr. L., a local oncologist. The genetic testing on the tissue sample indicated that there was a high rate of abnormalities counted and that I would benefit by having chemotherapy, then

radiation, then Tamoxifen. If I did all three, my chances of it returning inside of five years would be less than 10 percent. If I did not
do the chemotherapy, I had a greater than 20 percent chance of a
reoccurrence within the five years.

It is amazing, that by the participation of millions of women
who have gone before me in this same journey, that the experts can
state, with a high degree of certainty, whether a woman will benefit,
or not, from doing chemotherapy with an early-stage breast cancer,
therefore taking away the hesitancy and uncertainty of making the
decision on my own.

One month after the second lumpectomy and lymph node
biopsy, I started my first dose of Taxotere and Cytoxan. The date was
Friday, April 6, 2018. My mom drove me to the hospital. I sent her
home after we found out it would take four hours for the treatment.
No need for her to sit around staring at me for 4 hours.

I was premedicated with an antiemetic, a medication that con-
trols nausea and vomiting. It worked well throughout the treatments
as I had zero nausea issues. I declined the injection of Benadryl.
Honestly, I did not want to be knocked out and then embarrass
myself by snoring because of the sedation! Plus, I wanted to be able
to get up and out of there as soon as possible.

It all went uneventfully, and I called my mom to come pick
me up. I received a Neulasta injectable device. This is a device that
is placed on your arm and automatically starts an infusion of medication twenty-four hours after your chemotherapy. It helps keep
your white blood cells up after chemotherapy, which can be greatly
affected and cause you to be more susceptible to infection. In the
past, a patient would have to return to the doctor's office the day after
chemo to receive an injection of this medication.

I felt fine Friday, but Saturday, the fatigue hit. The next day
extending into the weekend is a blur. I felt like I passed out on the
sofa late morning. I awoke to a beeping and ticking sound and kept
thinking it was the garbage truck backing down our street, but it was
not garbage day. I could not wake up fully, and this noise kept repeat-
ing in my dream state. I also felt something on my arm and before
I could fully awaken, I had removed the adhesive of the Neulasta

device before the infusion was completed. The beeping and ticking were the timer on the device, like an alarm clock, signaling the start of the infusion over the next forty-five minutes. Oops.

I was told the side effects after this chemotherapy regimen should not be too bad and that I should be able to work. I had a full patient schedule for Monday morning. I did not feel great, but I got up, got the girls to school, and went to work. I was very tired, my body ached, and my head was pounding, and getting worse. I was having blurry vision that I attributed to the headache. I called the oncology office to tell them about the Neulasta device.

The staff were quite concerned and upset with my premature removal of the device and told me that I had to come in for a manual injection of the medication. I made my way to the hospital, just before noon. I struggled to get through the morning patients.

The infusion nurse asked how I was feeling. She did not like my responses and told me to "have a seat while I get the nurse practitioner." She then consulted Dr. L., and after getting the Neulasta shot, I was escorted to the Emergency Room for evaluation as my symptoms were not typical.

I had another CT scan of my head due to the headache and blurry vision along with some lab work. All was normal, I was instructed to see an eye doctor, and I was discharged. I canceled the rest of my work schedule for the week. I got an ophthalmology evaluation the next day that revealed my optic nerves were swollen, hence the blurry vision. The headache was a combination of the nerve swelling and migrainous reaction from the chemotherapy, even though I had taken oral steroids for three days in preparation for the chemotherapy.

It took me the rest of the week to recover, and three days of ice on my head to get over the headache. My vision improved over several days but did not feel back to normal. The eye doctor suggested a more prolonged taper of the steroids after the next infusion. The following week, I went back to work.

Three weeks later, I would need my second chemo infusion. First, I had to meet with Dr. L. to discuss options regarding the chemotherapy. I could stay the course and see how the side effects were and change the steroid dose. There was no way to determine if the side effects would be better, the same, or worse. The alternative was a different chemotherapy combination that would require a port or a Pic-line to be placed. Heart scans would need to be done as this agent was known to cause not only heart issues but a secondary form of blood cancer. My current chemotherapy could also cause this blood cancer but at a lower incidence, no heart issues, and a peripheral intravenous line was all that was needed. I opted to take my chances with the current treatment plan and wait to see how I reacted. I planned to have off the entire week following the next treatment though.

I was told that I would lose my hair. I was encouraged to research "cold caps" to help reduce hair loss during treatment. It was not covered by insurance and appeared to be quite a hassle without any guarantee of saving your hair. I opted to not use the cold cap therapy. It seemed too labor intensive. I would have tried it if the oncology unit had the infusion device for the caps, but since they did not have this equipment, I would have had to roll in a cooler with forty pounds of dry ice and change the cap often, before, during, and after the chemotherapy infusion.

The days leading up to the second infusion proved that I would indeed lose my hair. It was falling out in handfuls. Later that night, while making dinner, I found several strands of my hair in my dinner. That was disgusting, and I made the decision to have the girls help me shave the rest of my hair off. There was about a 1/3 of my hair left. When it starts to fall out, it falls out quickly. I tried to not make a big deal of it as Kaylee was already upset about the idea of her mom being bald and now was going to face the reality of it.

Making the decision to shave my head, instead of waiting another twenty-four hours for it all to finish falling out on its own, gave me a sense of control and empowerment. It is just hair after all, and it will eventually start to grow back. I knew this and kept saying it, but facing it in the mirror and not recognizing myself are quite different things. Hair is part of our identity and can be a security blanket, beside just being warmer. I often stated that it really did not matter, but deep down on a visceral level, it mattered.

Kiersten helped me shave if off, and Kaylee took pictures of it and then quickly left the room. Later, I found out she was afraid of what her classmates would say about her mom being bald and thought she would be a target for teasing. Neither of these things occurred and after a couple of weeks without any untoward incidents, just curiosity, questions, hugs, and prayers from her classmates, she became more relaxed about it, but admitted to hating the look.

In addition to being bald and cold, I also gained weight, and quickly. Most people lose weight when under treatment and that is usually the case, except in breast cancer. The chemotherapy agents are targeted at our female hormones since most breast cancers (but not all) are hormonally driven. And any woman knows that if you mess with these hormones, you gain weight. I gained just shy of thirty pounds during this period and half of it was water weight with pitting leg edema.

Exercise is, of course, always encouraged, and I have always been physically active, but the chemo fatigue combined with being a single mom was just not working in my favor for any additional physical exertion. The change in the steroid regimen helped. While steroids can also cause weight gain and fluid retention, in my case, it helped reduce it. They also gave me some energy and helped with the headaches and the vision changes.

The second chemotherapy infusion was uneventful. I drove myself this time as the side effects did not take effect right away. While I had the same symptomatology as the first dosing, it was not as severe. Either it was not such a shock to the system this second time or I was better prepared. Either way, I did not pull off the Neulasta injector and it was infused as it was designed to do. I did not have to worry about going to work. It took me until Wednesday (five days later) until I felt relatively normal again. By Thursday, I was fully functioning, tired but not as fatigued as before.

The ophthalmologist reexamined me after the second chemo dose and confirmed the optic nerves were still inflamed, hence the blurred vision, but my vision test was unchanged. He could not define how long this would last. I am now two years post-chemo-therapy, and the optic nerves are still "slightly" inflamed, enough for me to feel my vision is not as crisp as it was, but I still test the same on the vision chart.

I wore scarves or cute little hats on my bald head for warmth and to cover up the fact that I had no hair. It made the girls feel better about it and kept me warmer. As the weather got warmer, so did I. The chemotherapy killed my ovaries and put me into menopause prematurely. One day, I took Kiersten to her music lesson (drums) without my scarf. I did not plan on getting out of the car, or seeing anybody, so I left it at home.

The girls wanted to get a Slurpee from 7-Eleven on the way home, and I took them inside without thinking about it. Once inside, I realized I had no scarf. It was a defining experience. The man working the register was a big burly biker looking man. He looked at me as he rung up our order and with a fist pump told me, "You got this girl, go fight."

We were all encouraged, and to be honest, relieved. Kiersten remarked that he was "very nice to say that." We all left with smiles and a different attitude regarding my bald head. We realized that this is just part of the journey. I also realized that most people are going to see a bald Caucasian woman and know it was not a style choice but a treatment effect. There were so many people I encountered that encouraged me with a gesture, words, smiles, even gifts. I came to call them "God's lollipops," a term I stole from a patient. I define it as random people, through a kind word or gesture, that gave me a boost of sweetness on any particular day.

At work, I coordinated my head coverings with my outfits. Then the weather warmed up and the hot flashes took hold. I had to remove the head scarf while treating a patient because of an intense hot flash. She was one of my regulars, and I warned her before I took it off. I never put it back on or wore another one to work after that. Every patient I encountered, whether established or new, was so supportive or encouraging. More of "God's lollipop" moments.

Doses three and four of the chemotherapy, spaced three weeks apart went as smoothly as they could. The side effects were handled as best as I could manage them, and my work schedule was adjusted to meet my fatigue levels. I had a month free of treatments to heal and regroup before starting radiation therapy.

Chapter 37

My last infusion was June 29. I counted out three weeks and planned a shore vacation for me and the girls at the timeshare I bought at the Flagship in Atlantic City. I had been invited for the promotional sales pitch the November after Paul died and decided to check it out. Not something I would normally have agreed to, but we needed a break from the normal routine.

The facility had an indoor, heated pool, and I thought it would be a nice weekend away, something different to do for the weekend with the girls. We sat on the balcony of our room on the twenty-second floor with a blanket around all three of us, watching the waves roll in through the Brigantine Inlet, listening to the seagulls' squawk and the waves crash onto the jetty, spraying water into the air and smelling the fresh salt air. I did not realize just how much I missed being close to the saltwater.

We fell in love with the view and stayed for the sales pitch. After some negotiations, I bought the timeshare to be able to sit on a balcony with an ocean view whenever I wanted to get away for a day or a weekend or a week. Access to the boardwalk was just outside the front door, and it is a short drive to all the shore locations that we like to visit.

It was mid-July when we went for the week. Kaylee wanted to ride her bicycle on the boardwalk, as she saw so many doing when we had gone to Ocean City, New Jersey, the previous summer. I got a bike rack and attached it to the car and loaded the bikes, then had to rest! Everything exhausted me rather quickly. I had not counted on the accumulative fatigue effects of the chemotherapy.

It was extremely hot and humid that week. The heat and humidity, combined with the post-chemotherapy hormone changes, made me a sweating mess day and night. I did the best I could for the week, and we had a good time, but I was exhausted, day and night. I had to take naps in the afternoon and pace myself. The girls did their best to let me rest in between our excursions.

We rode bikes on the boardwalk every morning by 7:00 a.m. to be ahead of the heat of the day. We walked our favorite boardwalks and spent several days on the beach, with lots of sunscreen, especially for me. I took the kids to Cape May Zoo, and they did the Cape May Canopy Climb for a few hours. I attempted it, but halfway through, despite being clipped onto the wires, I thought I was just going to tumble out of the trees and not get up. I quit while I still had enough energy to drive us back to the hotel. We packed up a day early and came home. I needed the rest, and the kids missed their dogs.

While at the shore, there were more of "God's lollipop" moments. Two stand out well in my mind. One occurred with a group of women clapping at me as I walked past them on the boardwalk. I had no hat on and was wearing a breast cancer shirt. The second occurred as I came off the boardwalk and entered the restroom. I was hot and sweaty, but this woman insisted on hugging me regardless and wishing me well in my treatment.

I was still enrolled at graduate school. When I got the diagnosis of the breast cancer, I was in a dissertation preparation class. The next step was my dissertation work. I felt that I was too far into it to stop now.

I had prayed for guidance every step of the way with this graduate program. Every time a new health crisis emerged, I prayed about staying in school or dropping out. Funding for school? I prayed for a sign to withdraw or continue, and the next day the financial aid is approved. The brain tumor? Accommodations were made for the class and my missed online discussions were not penalized. God had gotten me this far in the program, and I prayed for the energy to complete it.

I did not want it to be my will to finish the program, but God's will for me. I wanted to know if this was still the right path for me. If it was or was not, I asked for a billboard with my name on it telling me the way I should go. It came in the way of my dissertation proposal being accepted, quickly followed by securing a clinical site for my project, through the guidance of my mentor, a fellow nurse practitioner and recent doctoral graduate herself.

There were many setbacks along the way at the clinical site, and it took all summer to get final approval to move forward with my project. I almost gave up and started looking for a new clinical site to perform the dissertation project. They were being exceedingly difficult and time and money for the next school quarter was being wasted. Through a phone call made by my mentor, it all ultimately came together, with apologies from the clinic's chief medical officer and their ethics committee.

Chapter 38

Midsummer, I received a letter from the State of New Jersey Pension Department that Paul owed a balance on a pension loan that I was not aware of. I thought someone had taken a loan out in his name fraudulently. I drove to the pensions office and waited an hour before I could speak to someone.

It was not a fraudulent loan. It was a loan he had taken out several years earlier but due to misfiled paperwork and a paperwork backlog, they were just getting around to processing it. This was a loan from Paul's employment at his municipal job.

The woman helping me was also a breast cancer survivor. Another "God's lollipop" moment. She was stunned when she learned that Paul was deceased and no one from pensions or the township had contacted me regarding his pension money. I did not know he still had a pension from the township as Paul had stated many times that there was an overlap of the pension systems between the township and his union employer.

This turned out not to be true. The two pension systems were different. I was to receive the balance of his vested pension monies minus the loan amount. She warned me that it would take a while to process the paperwork, and she was correct. It took several months, but I received a check for the balance just when I needed it. It was all about God's timing and provision, again.

In July, Kaylee was registered to attend a sleepaway camp at High Point Camp in Pennsylvania. This would be her first time away. She would be going with her cousin PJ. Peter and I drove the kids there together. They would be there Monday through Friday. Kaylee's dog, Morgan ended up dying the day before she returned from camp.

Morgan was a senior black lab that we took in for a friend. My friend was moving into new housing with her two girls and could not take Morgan with them. We knew Morgan, and she was a beautiful, friendly dog. My friend was moving into the new place in April. Paul and I had talked about taking in Morgan more than a year prior when my friend was looking for a new place to live, and the dog was posing an issue in finding a rental.

She called me early February, just before Paul died. She had been trying to find someone else to take the dog as she was fully aware of our situation but was having no luck. I told her I would take Morgan in April when she moved. I knew Morgan, being a senior dog, did not have a long lifespan ahead of her. I vowed that whatever time she had left to make it the best times of her life.

Kaylee's middle name is also Morgan. If I called her using her full name, it was interesting to see the dog respond first. Kaylee had an immediate bond with this dog. She spent many a night sleeping on the floor of her bedroom curled up with Morgan. When Morgan first came to us, we still had Opie and Lincoln, a mastiff mix. Opie died eight months after Paul had died.

I came home from work that Thursday afternoon. Fortunately, I had a light schedule and finished early. I found Morgan in my bedroom, half under my bed, covered in feces and urine. She could not stand and was dazed. She was in between seizures, but I did not realize that yet. I had just finished chemotherapy the month before and was still so weak that I could barely move her. I called Peter, my man for emergencies, and he came as quickly as he could. I called my friend to tell her what was happening, and she met me at the Vet hospital.

The dog never stopped seizing, even with valium. The vet suspected she had a brain tumor. We had Morgan just shy of eighteen months. We stayed with Morgan as she was euthanized. I dreaded bringing Kaylee home to another loss. I prayed to God for strength and guidance yet again.

When we got home Kaylee immediately called for her dog. I sat her down and explained what happened. This little girl, now eight years old, sobbed on her bedroom floor, in my arms for almost three hours before falling asleep in exhaustion. All her grief was wrapped up and let loose in this one episode. She cried for Paul; for the three hamsters, Oreo, Sunny, and Sugar; for Opie, and now, Morgan. It was awful. It broke my heart to see my little girl so broken. I prayed that God would ease her pain and help her heal.

We still had Lincoln, our Mastiff/Pyrenees rescue. He was rescued when he was six months old, and Opie was four at the time. By the fall, we were all ready to get another dog, and Lincoln needed a buddy. We visited our township animal shelter a few times. Then we attended their adoption day off-site and brought Lincoln with us. He met Luke on neutral territory and because Luke was a puppy, seemed to get along. Luke was a small black pit bull, possibly a Pit/Lab mix about seven months old. I think he is a pit bull mixed with chicken as he is afraid of everything and uses his nose to peck at everything. But he is cute and affectionate, and the two dogs got along fine once the hierarchy was established.

Chapter 39

After our vacation, I met with the radiation physician and had my tattoo dots placed for radiation. They are real tattoo ink and are permanent. They then had to add a few more in my armpit area. They form a Little Dipper constellation down my sternum, under the breast and into the armpit. I needed thirty-three radiation treatments, delivered daily, five days a week for six weeks.

I was not too worried about the treatments. I have cared for many patients over the years that had radiation to the head and neck areas during my years working in otolaryngology. Radiation to these areas is the worse as it causes loss of salivary glands and throat swelling necessitating insertion of a feeding tube in many cases. While I would have side effects from the radiation, they would be nothing compared to the experiences of my ENT patients.

My radiation treatments would be very narrowly focused to the right breast and right chest wall. My cancer was deep in the upper breast against the chest wall. I scheduled the treatments early in the morning and then would drive to work for the day. This routine worked out very well, and I felt fine for most of the weeks.

I had a second vacation planned during this summer. The second one took place in August. When I went to the Flagship for the sales pitch, my gift for staying for the presentation included four airfare tickets and a discounted book of places to stay. Together with my sister-in-law, Lori, we planned to go to Orlando for a week. We stayed at another time share community just outside of Disney. It was a private community with several pools and restaurants on the property. The vacation had been planned before I got the cancer diagnosis, and it took place in the middle of my radiation treatments.

The radiation oncologist was not too pleased about this break in the treatments, but she felt it would be okay. It would mean the treatments would take place over seven and a half weeks instead of six and a half weeks. I had completed the first three weeks of the radiation treatments by the time vacation arrived.

Until this time, I felt fine. During our two-hour plane ride, I started to fidget due to an uncomfortableness under the elastic of my bra on the right side. I had to keep adjusting the location of the elastic but did not get much relief. The "uncomfortableness" was now pain.

We landed in Orlando and arrived at the Resort. After a bit of a delay, we were able to get settled in our condominium. Once in the room, I pulled off my shirt to see what was wrong. The sixteen radiation treatments I had completed had caught up to me. My skin was blackened and blistered on the underside of the right breast around to axilla, or armpit area. I had radiation burns, and it hurt.

If I had not been on vacation, I am sure the radiation treatments would have continued despite the blistering. I had to liberally apply Aquaphor to the area, which I have come to love for my chronically dry hands. Aquaphor is what the radiation oncologist recommended I use to protect the skin during treatments, and I am glad I had remembered to pack it. The cool pool water was a balm to the burns. Amazingly, the skin healed quickly, and the blistering was gone within two days. The skin was peeling but no longer painful, only mildly annoying. By the end of the week, it was almost completely back to normal, with some mild redness remaining. We had a good time exploring the resort and its many pools. It was a very relaxing week, and I am so grateful Lori and my nieces and nephew were with me. I do not think I could have taken the girls by myself. Lori said she enjoyed it and found it relaxing too, but she is used to much busier vacations.

We returned home, and I had to finish the radiation treatments. I completed the remainder of the treatments the very end of August. I was hoping to be finished before the girls started back to school at the end of August. I did not want to juggle getting the kids to school, radiation treatments, and rushing to work. It turned out that I did not need to juggle it. Radiation ended one day before school started.

Then the fatigue of radiation caught up to me. It is strange how it hits you. I felt mildly tired one day and then terribly tired the next. It stayed that way, slowly improving over the next two weeks. Thankfully, it was not as debilitating as the fatigue from the chemotherapy.

I would be allowed a month to heal and recover and then start the oral medication Tamoxifen. It blocks estrogen uptake in the tissue to try to prevent a recurrence of the cancer. I was hoping to get off my seizure medication before starting the Tamoxifen. There is not any interaction between the two medications, but I was hoping to not have to be on it forever.

Chapter 40

I had an EEG performed (a test for seizures), which to the surprise of the neurologist, I passed. It showed no seizure activity which is unusual after the type of tumor and brain surgery I had had. The neurologist allowed me to taper down and off the medication over the next several weeks.

I was scheduled to start the Tamoxifen on Monday, October 1. On Sunday, September 30, I was getting ready to go to church. I went into the bathroom to finish getting ready and woke up confused, but I did not know that I was confused. I could not figure out what time church service started. I tried to look it up on the computer but could not coordinate what I was seeing as the start time, 9:00 a.m., with the current time of 10:10 a.m. A few minutes more and the brain fog started to clear. I had just awoken from a seizure and was "post-ictal." This term refers to the state of disorientation that occurs following a seizure. I had been unconscious for more than an hour.

I am so thankful the kids did not come looking for me and find me unconscious in the bathroom, again. I called the neurologist to inform her of what had happened and then I was back on the seizure medication, this time for life. I thanked God for allowing that seizure to happen while I was still home. Ten minutes later, and I would have been driving to church. At least I knew the medication worked well to control the seizures based on the EEG results and I would not have any issues with being allowed to drive.

133

I was told it would take six to twelve months after chemotherapy before I would feel back to normal again. I felt better at six months but not fully better until closer to a year. My hair started to grow back exactly three months after my last chemotherapy session. It came in darker than usual and started out very curly but got straighter as it grew out. Over the course of the next year, I slowly got the curls cut out. They were like baby curls in that sense and now I am back to my very straight hair, just a bit darker.

My eyebrows, however, are a different matter. They were the only bit of hair that survived chemotherapy. They thinned but never fell out fully; they have not grown back, either. They stayed their original hair color, which is a few shades lighter than my new hair color. No big deal as hair color is easy to change. I am thankful and happy to have hair back on my head. Whenever there is a discussion about someone's eyebrows, the girls make fun of me because I hardly have any.

Chapter 41

I started the Tamoxifen, and the first few weeks were easy. Then some of the aches and pains started. I was told that these would subside over time, and they have.

I had kept things as steady as I could for the girls since Paul died. I held to the same routine, with a lot of help from others, during my own battle. I needed a change because I had changed. My perspective on life had changed. I was starting to feel better, and I was getting restless.

I had talked about selling the house just before I had gotten diagnosed with cancer. It held so many memories and that is good, and bad. I felt stuck. I could not move forward in that house, and we desperately needed a second bathroom. The girls agreed about selling the house and listed their "wants" for a new house. A second bathroom was on all our lists. I needed a fenced-in yard, and I wanted a finished basement as I utilized our basement completely. It held the laundry room, pantry storage, my craft and exercise room and half of it was the kids play/gaming area. Kaylee wanted a pool. I told them that when I took down our Christmas decorations, I was packing up everything to get ready to sell the house.

I was still finishing up my doctoral dissertation project. My data collection had been completed in November. My paper was going through several edits for its final approval. In mid-December, I defended my project to the school via videoconference. I was now, officially, Dr. Schroeder, and received my diploma for my doctorate in nursing by the end of the month. I jumped and danced around the kitchen at the end of the presentation. The girls joined me in my celebration. It was a huge achievement, and I knew Paul would have been cheering with me, proud of my accomplishment.

Chapter 42

After Christmas, my plan was to de-clutter and pack up the non-essential stuff over the next six weeks and move it into a storage unit. I was able to do it in four weeks. I wanted to be able to get preapproved for a new mortgage while still holding my current mortgage, and again, I was able to do it. I had planned for at least three months of overlap but was hoping it would be less than that. I was still struggling with fatigue and wanted to be able to pace myself in moving out of the current home and into the new one.

I had found a home I really liked and in the neighborhood that I wanted as I was browsing the home listing websites. It was "the one," but it was only November. The houses in this neighborhood sold fast, and I knew it would not be available when I was ready to make my move. I kept looking just for fun and to see what was available in the surrounding areas.

I was ready to find a realtor a few weeks ahead of schedule, and the house I had my eye on from November had just been relisted, as the first buyer had fallen through. I looked at three houses just because I felt that I needed to look at more than one, but I knew in my gut this blue house was "my house." It was a blue colonial, fenced yard, with a garage and finished basement. And it had two full bathrooms, plus as Kaylee puts it, "a guest bathroom" which is a half bath on the main floor. The only box it did not check was the pool that Kaylee wanted. She will have to make friends with someone who has a pool in their yard! Another bonus, it was only a half mile away from Lori and Peter's home.

Before seeing the house in person, I had looked at the online pictures many times. I could already envision us living there. I had hoped for a house that I could host a Bible study group in and entertain a large family gathering. I had hosted family events in my current home, but as a small ranch-style home, it was cramped. I had never even thought about hosting a Bible study in the rancher due to space limitations, but in this other house, I would have the space for it. I could envision it too. I prayed that this was in line with God's plan for me. I made an offer, and after a little bit of negotiations, I got my blue house. I had initially planned a closing date sixty days out to allow me to get my house listed and sold, but the sellers wanted a thirty-day date. I agreed and I staged my house to be listed shortly after.

My rancher was listed, and it sold the same weekend it was listed, for full price. There were not a lot of houses available in the price point and size I had. They were either fixer-uppers or over $300K, so there was a lot of interest in my cute little home. I got my cushion of time that I had prayed for. I had two months to move out, clean it, and get the certificate of occupancy from the township. I would need all that time, and more, due to issues with the township. It was tedious, more tedious than loading the kids and dogs in the car and leaving during the realtor showings. There were several other delays, but eventually, it all got addressed and closing occurred a week after the original date.

Since Paul's death (which was now two years past), I had been selling a lot of the bigger and more expensive items of Paul's that were in the garage—table saws and other big power tools, an air compressor, a large power washer, boating gear and so much more. There was still a lot of stuff to get cleared out. I had held a yard sale during the prior summer, and I held another in the fall. Both were remarkably successful. Whatever did not sell, got donated. I took the rest of the boating stuff to the marina and let our friends take what they wanted, and the larger items, the marina owner bought from me. It was a nice and much-appreciated gesture from the marina owner.

Chapter 43

So much happened in such a short time, but this time it was good stuff. The year started out bad but ended on a positive note. I was past the hardest parts of my treatment. I would be maintained on the Tamoxifen for the next five years with frequent mammograms to start but tapering down to an annual mammogram after two years of clear mammograms on the affected side. I was cleared by my neurosurgeon and discharged from his care. My annual MRI of the brain showed no evidence of any reoccurrence of the brain tumor, and he was confident that it would not be returning after two years.

I tried to stay as true to a timeline in the recording of events as they played out, and I think I succeeded. The events around Paul are being told with his full permission to share his testimony. I am sure after this is done, I will recall some odd detail that I should have included, but there were a lot of things happening in quick succession. It is hard to keep it all straight at times. Some parts of this story do not have as much detail as I would have liked. It is because I either do not remember the exact details or it was too painful to expand on that specific event.

I had a patient tell me his wife was a kidney cancer survivor. He also told me they would argue about the emotional aspects of her cancer. He looked at it as "they were in it together." It was her diagnosis, but he was right alongside of her. She felt it was her body, her diagnosis, and therefore, she had sole ownership of it, and he could not understand the emotional part of it from her viewpoint.

When I asked Paul about this, he felt the same way. He owned the diagnosis and the changes in his body, and he lived with the fear, anxiety, and his fate of being terminally ill. I lived with it too. I lived with the fear and anxiety with him. I was going to be a single parent to two school-aged girls, so I was also facing the fate of his terminal illness. But I would be living, and he would not. It was not my body being ravaged with cancer, but his.

Being the spouse of the cancer patient and then myself being the cancer patient, I can tell you that both viewpoints are correct. We were in it together. But it was his body with the cancer, and his body undergoing changes and reacting to the meds. He was the one feeling poorly. I loved him and supported him and cheered him on. I was on the sidelines; he was playing the game. Then I got picked to enter the field and got to play too. I now understood the internalized feelings of being told I had cancer, undergoing the changes and side effects of treatment. I did not have a lot of fear and anxiety, and I was not terminally ill, but I did not feel well. I had no one to cheer me on. Well, I had people, friends, and family cheering me on, but it is not the same. My partner in life was not by my side supporting me and holding my hand. This thought trips me up anytime I think on it. This, and reliving his last twenty-four hours of life makes me sob. These were the most emotional parts of writing this book and where I just sat and cried as I had to relive those memories. I was angry that he was not with me, but I know that if there was any humanly way possible for him to have been with me, he would have been.

Chapter 44

Blessings

This is the chapter dedicated to the blessings through the trials. I have interwoven some of them in tiny pieces throughout the story, but now I can expand on the specifics of these blessings. And there were many, so this is going to be a long chapter. I am going to try to keep them in chronological order to keep in alignment with the chronological events already recorded. Robert Schuller stated, "I believe in the sun even when it is not shining, I believe in love even when feeling it not, I believe in God even when he is silent." I do not think God was silent during these years. I was not always listening or did not recognize the subtle nudges initially, but He was with me all along and His provision is evident in the positive things that happened in our lives.

It was a blessing that Paul was already mentally stable when he got the cancer diagnosis. If he had not already been in treatment, I am confident that his ability to cope with his diagnosis would have been much different to the point that I fear he may even have taken his own life if he were not on the correct medications to control his mood. His psychiatric nurse practitioner was amazing in her care and guidance for Paul's mental health. She did not take insurance, so it was self-pay for each therapy session. It was expensive but worth every penny.

It was God's provision that I was able to get him an appointment with the surgeon at HUP four days after getting his initial CAT scan results. It was an answered prayer that the surgery was successful and his recovery uneventful.

It was not our initial plan to go to MD Anderson in Texas, but that is where we went. From that visit, we were recommended a fabulous oncologist at Fox Chase. I will forever be grateful to Dr. P. for her professionalism, knowledge, encouragement, and care for Paul through this ordeal. She always had a plan when we came to his appointments after he was scanned. She truly was rooting for him even if she knew the odds were against him. The clinical trials he was able to participate in gave him hope. The urological surgeon at Fox Chase, Dr. U., was also professional during our encounters. He sent me a handwritten card stating, "It was my honor to be involved in Paul's care." I was touched that he made the effort, in his busy schedule, to send me a personalized note upon Paul's death.

Pastor Emmons and Graceway Bible Church sustained us spiritually and nutritiously. I cannot count the number of meals that were delivered to us through the years recorded in this book. The kids would be excited, looking to see who was bringing a meal on a particular night and what they cooked for us. The words of encouragement, cards, gifts, prayers, and hugs we received from members of my church were beautiful. We received money at times from various people too. The assistant pastor at the church, brought an envelope of money to the house one day after Paul's brain surgery. It was an odd amount, and I suspect somebody had given us the remaining monies of the benevolent fund. I was able to return that money, and then some, after Paul died to pay it forward for other people at the church.

My friend Jenn dropped gifts off to my house several times. They were not from her but from her own boss, a breast cancer survivor herself. Jenn and Renee took control of helping to plan our family celebration event the summer before Paul died. They both would text regularly to ask how we were. They did not require an immediate response and would follow up with me if they did not hear back after a few days. Their continual, nonintrusive support was lovely and much appreciated and remains today.

Pastor Emmons showed his *agape* love for us by ministering to Paul in the hospital during both of his kidney surgeries. Paul only attended church if Kiersten was performing with the children's choir, yet Pastor Emmons went out of his way to pray with him. He ultimately led him to accept Christ as his savior while recovering from his second surgery at Fox Chase. He continued to include us in his prayers throughout the years. He prayed over Paul when I got hospitalized with the brain tumor. He made regular visits to the house when Paul became too ill to attend church, and he baptized Paul a week before he died. He performed the service at Paul's funeral, and he continues to minister to us today.

We were blessed with time. As I stated in his eulogy, we were given an opportunity to plan and prepare in the three and a half years that he battled cancer. Many others are not given any time to prepare. He survived almost a year more than was average when he was diagnosed with the stage 4 cancer. The clinical trials he participated in may not have stopped his cancer and it did not seem like it slowed it down either, but it somehow prolonged his time here with us and for that, I am grateful.

God blessed us continually financially. I was able to formulate a plan for a savings account. Once that account was established, it just seemed to grow exponentially through work bonuses and tax refunds. We were able to go to Disney World twice during Paul's illness. We have wonderful memories to hold onto from those two trips. While I was out of work from my brain surgery, we did not struggle to pay our expenses. I was fortunate enough to hold both a short-term and long-term disability insurance policy. They more than replaced my paycheck during those nine months. We had people mailing checks to us, and of course, the money that the assistant pastor delivered. We had funds raised through the GoFundMe page that exceeded any expectations I had for it. God provided when I did not know what it was that we needed.

Faith Christian School/Faith Baptist Church also played a large part in our spiritual and financial health. During the surgeries, the school waived the monthly tuition until Paul returned to work each time. They continually prayed for us as a church and as a school. The students prayed for us. The teachers continually gave the girls extra hugs and love. Some of those teachers, specifically Ms. H. and Ms. G., also gave the kids rides home after school when neither of us could drive, or they delivered a meal or took the girls out for the day. Ms. W. and Mrs. G. played a huge role in Kiersten's life during second grade when Paul was first diagnosed. Ms. W. would continue to impact the girls as she later became Kaylee's third grade teacher and showered her with love.

All the teachers at that school, but especially the ones that the girls had for their classes, will forever hold an incredibly special place in our hearts. All the pastoral staff from the school/church, the teachers, and even some of the students and their families attended Paul's viewing or funeral service.

After Paul died, a pastor from the school, called me. He said, "Mrs. Schroeder, I do not know if you are aware of this, but we have a policy that in the event of the death of a parent of one of our students, we waive tuition for the next ten months [a full school year]." I was stunned. I did not know they had this policy. I mean who even has this kind of policy? Another blessing and a way for the school to keep the girls in a loving Christian environment while I figured things out financially.

The donation of services offered to us for our family celebration was humbling. It was truly astounding the generosity of complete strangers. They were willing to offer their services for whatever they could provide in their profession to help us. We did not accept many of those offers, but those that we did use, we are profoundly grateful. They made that day special and gave us the memories to live on in our hearts for many years to come. Racquel Marie Photography for her services and suggesting the GoFundMe page. She also sent the girls lockets with a picture of them during their respective father-daughter dances. Scarlet Creek Productions for the videography. Sal LoPresti, owner of Mannino's 3 for the food, Denise at VC Salon for the hair and nail services. Renee, owner of The Growing Place, for the girl's dresses, her love, and support. She was another friend who constantly reached out to check on me, never with any pressure or expectations, just friendship. Renee and Jen from church for securing the church and pastor's schedule, as well as overseeing the entire event. I love you both dearly for your friendship and generosity of giving.

My workplace and boss, James A. Boozan, MD. Everyone was supportive during these years and were my cheerleaders. The staff organized some fundraisers for me. We had done this before for the office manager who later succumbed to her own cancer, but now, the staff did it for me. Some of it they kept secret, but some of it I knew about. They presented me with money after Paul's death. They had raised a few thousand dollars by selling popcorn and white rubber cancer bracelets. The patients donated generously when they found out what the fundraiser was for. It was amazing and humbling, and I am amazed at the love that was displayed for us.

Paul's workplace was equally amazing. I mentioned previously that his boss, G, kept Paul employed to secure his benefits. I do not want to specifically name his workplace as I do not know if his former boss would get into trouble for his efforts. It allowed Paul, while on a reduced work schedule to keep a full paycheck, his health insurance as well as a life insurance policy. This office was in the process of being consolidated when Paul entered hospice. Paul died two weeks before this office closed, and his boss "forced" into retirement. Two more weeks and we would have been scrambling for health coverage as I did not carry any, yet. It was a risk G took to help us, and I am forever grateful to him, as well as the support of Paul's coworkers. They too showered us with love, prayers, and occasional meals.

Paul has a daughter from a relationship that occurred before we had gotten engaged. She was adopted by her stepfather as a toddler. She never knew Paul (or that she had been adopted) until she became an adult even though Paul remained in contact with her mother and watched her grow up from a distance. During this time, he was able to reconcile with her and spend time with her newborn son, his grandson. We all spent time together during his last Christmas, at a tree lighting ceremony in Bordentown. Paul dressed in many layers, five I think, to be able to be outside for a prolonged time. He was about to fall over from fatigue, but he persevered to create memories. He did not want to waste a single moment he had left.

We were blessed in having time to prepare for end-of-life events. We were given a gift of time, not that Paul had a long life, but time to prepare for his death. Not everyone is so lucky to have time to prepare and "get your affairs in order." I like to think we used that time well. We were able to get wills created through the connection of our former sister-in-law Maureen. We had funeral services well planned, thanks to Gary, our neighbor and funeral director. A former patient, Jim, owned a catering business at Mercer Oaks Golf Club. He insisted on providing the meal for the repast. It was delicious. Then Mrs. Z. got involved and assisted in contributing to the cost of the food.

My rearranging of the basement before discovering the brain tumor was a blessing. It was a nice surprise to see how organized the basement was after my brain surgery. It also made finding the "important papers" simple. In hindsight, I know the urge I had to clean that area, as well as the sense of urgency I had during the summer to finish the end-of-life planning with Paul, came from God. I cannot explain it any other way.

It was an answer to prayer that Paul was able to get the boat engines installed and running the summer of 2016. It was another answer to prayer that we were able to sell both the boats quickly and before Paul died. He genuinely wanted to have "things settled" before his death and not leave me burdened with anything extra. I think we accomplished that. While I found it strange that Paul wanted to set me up with another man before he died, it was a blessing that he gave me the freedom to move on and date and remarry when I felt the time was right. He wanted me to be taken care of and loved and not to have to do everything alone.

Then there was the fundraiser dinner put together and hosted by Women With A Purpose. I knew nothing about this organization, but apparently, many others did. I do not even know how it was advertised to draw so many people. The organizers had planned on 100 people, which included their normal attendees and participants of the organization plus my head count for family members.

The additional 100 plus people were parents and students from the kids' school and some additional church friends and some friends of friends who spread the word around.

One of our deacons from the church is also a financial advisor. I did not know him before Paul's death, and I therefore did not know his profession. He came highly recommended by Renee. I explained to him how I wanted to invest the life insurance, and he understood completely. He came up with a few categories and ideas for the funds and has been a trusted advisor since. I used a travel agent from church, to book the Disney cruise. My financial advisor contacted her and had a gift bag awaiting our arrival in our stateroom as a sweet surprise for our trip.

It was a blessing that the girls and I were able to travel after Paul's death. Besides investing the life insurance money for the girl's future, I used some to have fun. The trip to Universal Studios was relaxing and fun, even though bittersweet. We want to return there soon. The Disney Cruise was healing. We have another already booked, but the pandemic of 2020 delayed it. Even our short stay in Ocean City, before the summer came to an end, was soothing to our souls. The visit and buying of the timeshare at the Flagship, while not really an investment, was a way to ensure we make time to slow down and enjoy the Jersey shore every year.

During our Disney cruise, Patrick, Peter, and their best friends remodeled our bathroom in the rancher. It still had a blush pink tub! They took it down to the studs and had it completed during the week we were on the cruise. I had purchased the supplies, and they did the labor. It came out amazing and was a nice plus to selling the house a year later.

After Paul stopped driving, and before he died, my car started to have problems. It was nine years old. Paul told me to trade both our vehicles in for a new car. It was hard to do it. It took me a week of negotiating with the salesman to finalize the deal. The salesman came to the house to drive Paul's truck back to the dealership. I cried the entire way as I drove my own car to the dealership. It was his truck in the rearview mirror, but it was not him driving it, and it would be the last time I would see it. Afterwards, it was a blessing to have traded it in. I was not going to keep it, and the two vehicles gave me a nice trade-in value. And if Paul's truck was not in the driveway, then he was not home. This helped me tremendously after his death. If his truck was in the driveway, no matter how much time would have passed, I would have opened the door to the house and expected to find him there. When I drive through that neighborhood and go past that street, I still look for the truck in the driveway even though I tell myself I am just looking to see how the new owner is maintaining the house.

I cannot find a blessing in my own cancer diagnosis, but I was blessed in having peace about my treatments. I was calm, and that was God's doing, not mine. I have confidence and a hope for my future; again, God's provision. I did what I had to do to give me the best chance of survival, and I have come out the other side of those treatments, cancer-free.

I was chosen as a recipient of a free photography session by Jackie Murphy Photography during my cancer treatment. The pictures came out well, I just do not particularly like the way I look in them due to the weight gain and baldness. They are part of my journey and my story.

The "God's lollipop" moments that came at unexpected times that lifted my spirits were another blessing. They encouraged me and my girls and put smiles on our faces.

God answered my prayers for a fast sale of my home and the purchasing of my new home. He has helped me fulfill my desires for that home in having Bible studies and groups from church over for fellowship. My church has a ministry to help people, especially widows, move. There were many hands available that weekend, most from my church but also friends from the kid's school.

I have also hosted those family gatherings at my new home. Only now, it is to try to keep our Schroeder family traditions alive. Pop Schroeder passed away in 2019. He suffered from Alzheimer's and was declining. He passed away, suddenly, in his sleep while at the nursing home. It was fast, painless, and peaceful. Anything anyone could have hoped for. The only downside was mom was not at his side. She, too, was in the nursing home but in a different unit. His funeral gave honor and recognition to his service to the community as a police officer, and councilman within our town.

I have made amazing friendships. Those that I called friends, fell away. Those that were on the outskirts of my circle, became part of the inner circle. They texted or called to check in and remained steadfast in their outpouring of support and love. Renee D., Jen, Renee M., and Karan P. immediately come to mind. Friends from the marina, Karen and Jack, helped during the family celebration event. Karen also made the hour-long drive several times to sit with me while I was in the hospital. She was with me at the house when I got the call from my oncologist with the pathology results from my surgery. They also took the girls on occasion for a fun day out. There were families from school who featured heavily in the girl's lives. The grandmom of these families, Xiomara, babysat the girls for many years during the summer. She is another adopted grand-mom in our lives. We are still friends with these families today, the Johnson, Botteri, and Brumbach families.

My family did offer to help, but I did not accept help from them initially. Their relationship with Paul was not loving or accepting, but always judgmental. Now that he is gone, they talk about him as if he is the greatest thing since sliced bread. I could not have my mom sitting with Paul during his periods of confusion, as I did not think he would take comfort from it in his moments of clarity. My mom was a source of support during other times. She does not do well with spontaneous gestures of help but does great when tasked with a specific request.

Lori, Peter, and Patrick were my go-to family for our needs. Patrick was a great help with a bunch of different things. He filled in the gaps when needed. Sometimes he felt like he was not doing enough and was relieved to be able to assist in whatever way he could. Our former neighbor, and honorary grandmom, Mom-Mom Mirinda has been such a beautiful blessing in our lives through the past sixteen years. She loves my girls as her own and attended all the girls school performances. We were sad to move away from her, but she is not too far away. I feel that grandparents can offer such love and wisdom to children and you can never have enough of them in your life. That is why we have collected two additional grandmoms beside their biological ones. A third set of grandparents will enter our lives in 2019.

Lori and Peter were constantly holding us up and together when the crap hit the fan. They feature predominantly in this story. I cannot even begin to express my deepest love and gratitude for all that Lori and Peter did for us. They lived close to us and were able to arrive quickly when needed. Lori's connections at the local hospital helped smooth the way through several medical events. Peter's availability, because he was not working, made him readily available for too many things to remember.

Then there was the doctorate program. I prayed my way through every class, every week. I had so many doubts about starting it and then staying in it. I had guilt about it too. Even though Paul urged me to enroll and complete it, I felt selfish for the time it took from him and the family. I did my schoolwork at the kitchen table while the girls did theirs. I was able to do a lot of the classroom discussions during my lunch break at work. Finishing it, while difficult, was a promise I made to Paul and a true accomplishment. Every time I prayed, questioning the decision to enroll in the next class, God would open a door pertaining to school. Usually in the way of funding or completion of a project.

Shortly after moving into the new house, the check from Paul's pension arrived. It had been four months since I made that visit to the pension office. It was more than I expected and arrived just as I was setting up my payback plan for the student loans. I still have a balance on the student loans, but it reduced the amount by two-thirds.

Kiersten had asked me, "Why is God letting such bad things happen to us?" This was before Paul died but after our respective brain surgeries. I gave her the only answer that I could. I did not know why these things happen. Or why the bad things happen in multiples. But despite the bad stuff, there were a lot of good things too. I reminded her of the love being shown us by the community, the neighbors, the school, and the churches. The good things that were occurring that we did not ask for, but they just happened. That was God, taking care of us while we were in the valley.

Epilogue

We are surviving, but I would not say we are thriving. We did not come out of these experiences unscathed. I am cancer-free but have aches and pains that did not exist before. I am sure many who are reading this can relate. I never regained my full stamina for physical activity after the brain surgery. The inflammatory effects of chemotherapy did not help with that in any way. I still get a lot of things done and exercise regularly, but my types of exercise had to change to accommodate my body. I was hurting myself trying to do the high-intensity aerobic workouts I was previously used to doing. I can still do my spin bike, but it is at less intensity and not always the full workout. The high-intensity workouts are now modified to lower-impact aerobics, and I started Pilates, mixed with some yoga.

After reading a story about a red envelope placed in the Christmas tree as a tribute to a father's death, we created our own red envelope for Christmas. It represents the donation made to Fox Chase in Paul's honor. I also make one on his birthday and Father's Day and will continue to do so going forward, hoping that it can improve someone else's "tomorrows."

The girls seemed to do well initially. Then teenager girl hormones hit Kiersten. She started cutting herself. Because of Paul's mental health issues and his parents not seeking the proper psychiatric help for him, we had vowed together, when Kiersten was born, that any child we have will receive mental health care at the first sign of trouble. It was another thing we had talked about before he died. We expected the girls to have issues with grief. We did not know how much they really were able to understand about Paul's illness or the permanency of death. They were only eleven and seven at his death. Kiersten of course was able to understand it better than Kaylee.

Paul's death disillusioned Kiersten in her faith. It has taken her a few years to regain a relationship with Christ. She knew God hears our prayers and "anything asked in My name will be answered." She did not understand how her dad could have died when so many people had been praying faithfully for him to be healed. She lost her glowing aura, and her smile was dimmed. She was diagnosed with moderate depression, anxiety, and PTSD. She was almost thirteen. She was started on an antidepressant, which greatly helped. After a year of therapy, we discussed tapering her off.

I did not know she had stopped taking them and she was hoarding them in her room. Then I found a suicide note. I had just completed a continuing education course on suicide screening in the ER as part of my annual education requirements. All this information was fresh in my mind when I found the note. The entire circumstances of the course, where Kiersten had placed her notebook and the timing of me finding it were all God's doing. In addition to the suicide note, she had a plan. It was a plan that would have been successful. She is now attending twice weekly counseling sessions in addition to seeing her psychiatry provider for medication management. She is now doing much better. Her mood is stable, and she has become very active in church and the worship band. I am extremely proud of her. She is maturing into a beautiful, smart, young lady.

While this was happening, I got Kaylee back into therapy. I was afraid that while I was distracted with Kiersten that something with Kaylee was going to sneak up behind me and bite me on the butt. She had also attended therapy for a while but was discharged as she seemed to be doing well, but in hindsight, she was not. She is not good at expressing her feelings and tends to push them down to not cry, which embarrasses her. Her grief was coming out in anger, and it was directed at her big sister. She, too, had anxiety. She expressed being afraid for me every day. She was afraid when I left the house that something bad would happen and I would not return. Kaylee had also started cutting, but her episodes were more scratches on the surface. She recently disclosed to her therapist she thought about taking pills. We escalated her therapy to an intensive outpatient group which she is just completing. I am very proud of her progress, too. She is thriving in her school and has become involved in the church youth group and worship band too. She, too, is growing and maturing into a beautiful and smart young girl.

While I was getting ready to sell my house, I met a man at church. He had started attending shortly after Paul had died. We did not officially meet until January 2019. He helped me get the house ready by addressing the issues to get the certificate of occupancy. We got married later that same year. I figured if he could be interested in me while I had little hair, was bloated from the chemotherapy, and was not scared off by hearing some of my story, then he was a keeper. He checked off every one of my mental boxes for what I would be looking for in someone for my future if I had the opportunity to date and remarry. The timing was uncanny. I had just expressed to the wife of my pastor, that I was in a good place to think about dating again and was open to the possibility if it presented itself. The following Sunday, Ed was waiting for me by the doors of the church sanctuary. I laughed at him as his thought for dating was someone with older children and no pets. Ha, he got two school-aged girls, two dogs, and two guinea pigs. He has two children, both young adults, from a prior marriage. It has been an adjustment for all of us, and we are growing as a family. He now claims my girls as his own and takes his role as stepdad seriously. He loves us and has become the partner for me that Paul wanted me to have as well as father figure for his girls. His parents include my children as their grandchildren, hence, another set of grandparents. My family, however, have set their minds and hearts against Ed. We pray for them daily since that is all that we can do. Because Paul had expressed his desire for me to remarry and to live, I was able to date and marry Ed without the feeling that I was betraying Paul. It was truly a blessing to have that peace and freedom to move forward.

Through this journey, I have a few things that I can tell you what not to say to someone during a trial or death of a loved one. As a Christian, I do not need you to quote scripture to me, as it is usually out of context of what it is written in the Bible. Unless you can tell me exactly what the plan is that God had/has for me, do not tell me "God has a plan!" I believe He did and does have a plan for me, but at that point in my life, hearing that phrase just made me angry.

Do not try to offer comfort by sharing a similar story, regardless of whether it had a positive ending. It appears like you are downplaying my issue or not hearing me well.

Do not ask me what I need or what you can do for me. I did not know at that moment what I needed or wanted. Oftentimes, even if I did need something, I probably would have told you I was fine. A wise woman at church, Renee, knew this about me. She instructed me to nod my head yes and say, "Thank you, that would be lovely," to anyone who offered any type of help in any way, regardless of what it may have been. Do not offer, as it gives the receiver a chance to decline. Just take charge and drop a meal off to the house, send a card or leave a message on the phone.

Forgive me if I was short with you when you asked for updates. Maybe I was very tired and did not want to talk about the cancer that day. Or there may have been ten people before you that I already relayed the information to, and I was tired of talking about it. Sometimes being able to talk about what was going on helped, but other times it increased my anxiety. Be cognizant of this and offer hugs, prayers, and support to those who are struggling with their own issues.

It is okay if you do not know what to say. It is also okay to tell me that. Approach me, tell me I do not know what to say. Tell me you are thinking about me, praying for me. Just give me a hug as a show of love and comfort. Any of these gestures are and were appreciated.

I had done a lot of reading during my cancer year, looking for comfort and inspiration. I latched onto some biographies and autobiographies. I laughed my way through Rick Rigsby's *Lessons I Learned from a 3rd Grade Dropout*. I marveled at Martin Luther King's grace, humility, bravery, intelligence, and godliness. I read some information on Mahatma Gandhi. I cried through Randy Pausch's *The Last Lecture*. His words and his will to fight his pancreatic cancer at age forty-six, to survive for his wife and children echoed so much of

Paul's battle, it was uncanny. I read Amy Robach's *Better,* her autobiography after her breast cancer battle, trying to find inspiration and hope during my own breast cancer batter. I enjoyed them all and learned something from each one of their stories.

Through reading others' stories, I had an epiphany that God was using me to be an example in honoring Him. I do not know the full extent of what He has planned for me or how I will be used, but I know that the combination of my nursing career, being the caregiver to my spouse with cancer and being a cancer survivor myself, gives me a unique professional and personal perspective in this lived experience. Perseverance is not enduring a long race but enduring many smaller races one after another (Walter Elliott), and I feel that I have certainly persevered through these few years. Maya Angelou stated that, "people will forget what you say, people will forget what you did, but people will never forget how you made them feel."

It has been a journey to share this story. It is a blessing and an honor to be able to keep Paul's memory alive by sharing his testimony, by giving him a voice beyond the grave. It is my sincerest hope that I made you feel something with this testimony. I pray that I inspired you, gave you courage and strength. I pray I gave you hope for a better tomorrow and knowledge that you can persevere and come out the other side to not just survive, but to live, smile, love and laugh again.

Eulogy

Paul and I have been married for twenty-two years. Paul and I first met in junior year of high school. It was NOT a love match; in fact, we could not stand each other, and my mom would probably have been happy if it stayed that way. He was a grease monkey that somehow ended up in my honors physics class, and I was a snob with a tight short, permed hair do! Clearly, if he was in my physics class, he was not the average grease shop monkey. We had a mutual friend who knew the family well and she said he was a nice guy, so I gave him some benefit of the doubt and lowered myself to talk to him in class. He was a clown, always with a joke, quick-witted and sarcastic and too serious about anything, but otherwise, harmless. A bit crazy and off-the-wall with some of his antics and things he would say that sometimes made people a bit leery of him. But then, if you got to know him, you realized that he had a strong sense of morals, of what was right and fair and just and fought for the underdog and would help you out in a pinch, anytime, anywhere. He was smart, very smart, and very handy to have around. Had every tool imaginable and knew how to use them too. And he became my best friend and confidante that I married in 1994.

Through my family, he got introduced into the world of boating and became obsessed with the hobby to point that it took precedence over everything else at times. He delved into all aspects of it and became involved in teaching safe boating classes and advanced boating classes through the USPS, and it was our escape with our dogs every weekend—and you all know how we like our dogs—regardless of the weather for many years. We have had several boats and named them *Miss Guided* as so many thought we were crazy for not getting a house and settling down. But I was still working on my degrees, and he supported me through my school journey, even now as I am finishing a DNP. We were young, immature, footloose, and fancy free with nothing to tie us down yet, so we enjoyed ourselves. And I am glad we did because life only gets harder, and after two children and into our nineteenth year of marriage, life threw us a big curveball.

In 2013, he got diagnosed with cancer, and while it is a terrible disease to be diagnosed with, it helped to make him a better person over the past three plus years. He reprioritized his blessings in life; got help from a wonderful psych NP who stabilized some of his very turbulent mental emotions; he became a more attentive and loving and kinder husband and become more present in the moment with his kids. We made some good memories for the kids the past three summers—two Disney trips and the vow renewal family celebration event. It is sad that it takes such a diagnosis to make a person realize what is truly important in this life, but it did give him time to realize what was important in his life, and he took advantage of the opportunity to make personal adjustments, fix some regrets, make amends for past issues, and make memories with his family. Not everyone is so lucky to be given that opportunity or do not take advantage of the opportunity.

While there will forever be missed opportunities and regrets in life, we must make the best of what we have here and now and appreciate the bad trials, as they may be hidden blessings in the end. This journey, if nothing else certainly taught Paul and I that, as well as those around us. Through these trials, especially the past year with my brain surgery, then Paul's brain surgery and his progressive decline afterwards, we became a stronger, closer family. The kids saw what the true meaning of the marriage vow of "in sickness and in health" really means, and they saw the outpouring of love of a community, church, and family that came together to pull us through a really tough year in 2016. We became humble in many aspects as we had to accept help in caring for our family as we could not care for ourselves at times. Despite the hardships, we have also been thoroughly blessed in other aspects of our lives and in ways we could not imagine and did not know we needed.

Paul did come to accept his fate, turned to prayer, and was grateful and respectful of the spiritual guidance he received from Pastor Emmons. He was interested the past few months in 2 Corinthians 5:1 where the apostle Paul talks about our earthly tent (or body) being torn down in order to receive our godly tent in heaven. Kaylee, in her eight-year-old simplicity, summed Pastor Emmons discussion with Paul in about thirty seconds saying: "When you get to heaven, you get a new body—no cancer, no pain. We cannot see/hear you, but you can see/hear us, and we will see you again, but not for a long while." Verse 8: "To be absent in the body, we are present with the Lord." Our faith allows us to believe that Paul has received his heavenly body and is present with the Lord. I know that my family takes great comfort from this belief. His motto of "never surrender" became his mantra for survival and inspiration for others to continue their fight in their own personal trials. He is very loved and will be forever missed.

Rest in peace, and enjoy your new heavenly tent, Paul. We love you.

Senior prom, 1989

Wedding day, 1994

First Disney trip, 2014

Disney, 2015

The "little" boat

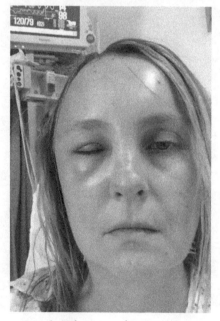

2016, 2 days post brain surgery

Christmas 2015, Patrick, Paul, Peter and Mom

Family celebration event, 2016

Father-daughter dances

Summer camping trip, 2016

Christmas 2016

January, 2017, Kaylee's birthday

Universal trip, 2017

Disney Cruise, 2017

Lori and I at Garth Brooks concert and then
Casting Crowns with Kiersten, 2017

Summer 2018, Photo session by Jackie Murphy

Doctoral graduation, March 2019 with my mom

Summer 2020. Ed, Kiersten, me and Kaylee

About the Author

Cathy Jo Schroeder-Soden is a family nurse practitioner and an assistant professor of nursing in New Jersey. She has been a nurse since 1992, receiving her associate in nursing from Mercer County Community College. She earned her Bachelor of Nursing from Stockton State College in 1997. She completed her family nurse practitioner/master's in nursing degree at Hahnemann University in 2000 and her Doctor of Nursing practice from Capella University in 2018. She is a native of New Jersey and resides there with her family and several rescued pets. She likes boating, fishing, crafts of all types, and reading, and volunteers with a large dog breed rescue group as well as her local church.

CPSIA information can be obtained
at www.ICGtesting.com
Printed in the USA
BVHW051703071222
653678BV00005B/225